This
Polish Blood
in
America's Veins

The author has also compiled his war memoirs entitled, *Unbookish and Undivulged Story of World War II.*

THIS
POLISH BLOOD
IN
AMERICA'S VEINS

*Sketches from the life of
Polish immigrants and their descendants in America,
illustrating a part of American history
unknown to most Americans*

MIECZYSLAW W. FRIEDEL

VANTAGE PRESS
New York Washington Atlanta Hollywood

English version corrected and condensed in 1977 from the
original memoirs written in Polish in 1961-64.

FIRST EDITION

Copyright © 1978 by Mieczyslaw W. Friedel

Published by Vantage Press, Inc.
516 West 34th Street, New York, New York 10001

Manufactured in the United States of America
Standard Book Number 533-03203-2

Dedicated to my grandchildren,
Chris and Gary,
to acquaint them with
their ancestry

I am indebted to my dear sister, Alina Markowski, former Registrar of the University of Toledo, Ohio, for her advice and typing.

Table of Contents

This
Polish Blood
in
America's Veins

I

Introduction

Many years have gone by since, as a young immigrant from Poland, I zealously particpated in Polish-American activities, being a Polish-language newspaperman, actor, organizer of theatrical, educational, and civic groups, and director of radio programs.

I don't want to compare myself to the world's great philosophers and thinkers, who chose to run away from their previous life into faraway deserts or mountains to meditate and "find themselves"; to look at the world from a perspective and find a new philosophy.

However, I've separated myself similarly from the previous activities, preoccupied with the Polish-American world upon joining voluntarily the United States Army in World War II.

Faraway from the Polish-American communities were the army camps in Texas, Georgia, the Blue Ridge Mountains of Maryland, the preinvasion bases in England and Wales, the foxholes in France, Normandy, and Brittany, the bunkers and shelters on the Siegfried line, the towns and villages of Belgium, Luxembourg, Germany, and Czechoslovakia.

There I had ample opportunity to meditate over America and my work in Polish-American communities; separated many

1

degrees from the mainstream of American life. From this perspective, I began to distinguish the trees from the forest and the forest from the trees.

I was lucky to survive the war and return unharmed to the United States of America.

Looking at and listening to what was going on among the so-called American Polonia, I got the impression that I came back to backward, medieval people, unaware of the great happenings and changes that shook our world, although here and there I detected bright rays trying to pierce the curtain of parochial Polish-American regression.

Fresh in my war memories were still the scurrilous, dirty, insulting propaganda leaflets strewn on the battlefields by Nazi artillery and air force, directed against our commander in chief, President Roosevelt, with the objective: to discredit him, undermine the confidence and loyalty of American soldiers to the President of the United States, and influence their overseas votes at presidential election time. I couldn't bear to listen to similar parrotlike insults, attacks, and arguments repeated by undiscriminating, thoughtless Polish-Americans and emanating mostly from their mediocre leaders and politicians trying to swing the Polish vote from the Democratic to the Republican side, or gain moral and financial support for the so-called Polish government in London.

These attacks, accusations, and even vulgarities pertaining to our late President Roosevelt, his wife, and supporters of his ideology are being spread until this day among the Polish-American people and Polish-language press, and are inspired by certain vicious, hate-mongering circles, claiming to be ultra-patriotic Poles. Among their victims was a great American friend of the Polish people and nation, the late Mr. Patterson, editor of the *Toledo Blade*. The *Milwaukee Journal* also was subjected to their ire because it printed objective news or articles about postwar Poland. Usually in whispers or innuendos, they were striving to convince other Polish-Americans that papers like the *Milwaukee Journal*, printing anything favorable to Poland were dangerous, radical, and pro-Communist papers.

Sinister attitudes were directed against individuals (Polish or non-Polish) who dared to voice a sympathetic or friendly opinion about the postwar Polish state.

There was a time when Polish-Americans who went to Poland to visit relatives, to see conditions in the country with their own eyes, were denounced as traitors or pro-Communists. These accusations subsided after prominent Americans, members of the United States Congress, and even Presidents Nixon and Ford paid friendly visits to Poland.

Utterly disgusted, I decided to refrain from participation in that sphere of Polish-American life, which was dominated by a Machiavallian political machine, trying to make it a separate entity removed from the mainstream of American life. However, I remained a studious observer and was able to capture many details pertaining to the life of millions of Polish-Americans.

Since I came to the United States in 1911, at the age of fourteen years, I've passed through three important stages of assimilation.

In the first stage, I considered myself a temporary inhabitant of the United States of America. I was happy to come here and see America—but I didn't arrive here on my own accord. I came with my parents and sisters. My dream was to return someday to a free, independent Poland, which at that time was partitioned and ruled by Russia, Germany, and Austria. At the age of twelve, I was active in the Polish underground movement as a student in a gymnasium (high school) in Polish Silesia, embraced by the Austro-Hungarian empire. My father was a fighting Polish journalist, editor, and publisher of the *Voice of the Silesian People*. My mother was engaged in patriotic theater groups.

During World War I, I joined, with over 20,000 other volunteers from the United States, the Polish Army in France, serving in Canada, France, Poland, and Ukraine (Polish-Russian War, 1919-1920).

Second stage: The United States government, which had sanctioned our volunteer enlistment contracts in the Polish

Army in France, regarded as an ally in the war with Germany, directed that we be released and sent back to the United States. Accordingly, I was released with many other volunteers from America at the Ukrainian front and returned to America on a U.S. transport ship.

Disgusted with conditions I had seen in Poland, I decided to remain in America. I obtained United States citizenship and disavowed loyalty to Poland, but as a Polish-American journalist I tried to advise the people of Poland what kind of government they should have, basing my opinions on democratic conditions in America and separation of church and state. I also contributed to causes fighting for the establishment of such conditions in Poland. On the other hand, I was interested in American politics and contributed to domestic progressive, democratic causes. My other civic interests were endeavors to abolish discrimination against people of Polish descent and help the Polish-American youth, a large majority of which, in my opinion, was drifting aimlessly, especially during depression times, often ashamed of its national descent, not realizing that Polish heritage offered them a rich, cultural background.

Third stage: Realization of the paradox of double personality. After voluntary service in the U.S. Army during World War II, I regard myself strictly as an American, naturally of Polish descent, and I'll never hide it or be ashamed of it. All Americans, except maybe Indians or Eskimos, have a foreign origin and that doesn't make them better or worse Americans; although certain people, mentally backward or chauvinistic, look upon citizens of Slavic or other non-Anglo-Saxon descent with an air of superiority or contempt.

In my opinion, the blood which flows in America's veins is mixed. It's a conglomeration of all blood types, peculiar to all racial and national classifications. As an American I am not sticking my nose in the internal affairs of other countries or nations, including Poland. However, I freely admit my affection, my interest, and well-wishing for the Polish nation. And since I know its language, history, suffering of its people, and martyrdom of the nation throughout the centuries, naturally, I would like to acquaint my fellow Americans with the nation of my origin, its history, struggles, and accomplishments.

As far as discrimination against Americans of Polish descent is concerned—in this third and final stage of my American assimilation, I continuously and strongly resent it—but I differ in this respect with quite a number of fellow Polish-Americans. That is, I am against discrimination and for equal civil rights for ALL Americans, regardless of race, nationality, or religious beliefs or disbeliefs.

In writing these sketches about Polish-American life, I do not pretend to be a chronicler or historian. I am recording simply my own observations and experiences, and the experiences of others as they were told to me or written in newspapers and books. No doubt the life of Polish people in America could be pictured in brighter or darker colors, wider or narrower scope, in a more critical or more glorifying form, depending on one's experiences, viewpoints, and perceptions.

My critical observations pertaining to certain aspects of Polish-American life are not intended to diminish important contributions of Polish people and their descendants to America. These contributions, past and present, are recorded in history.

But I hope that my sketches will help us all in America to get better acquainted and to bring out things of which even many Polish-Americans are not aware. And maybe the young generation of Americans will be able to learn more about the old generation of immigrants in America.

II

Characteristics and Approximate Number of People Of Polish Blood Living in America

In the beginning of the twentieth century, when Poland was occupied and ruled by Russia, Germany, and Austria, the Polish people in the United States were looked upon as a "Second Poland," and the city of Chicago, with the second largest Polish population at that time (400,000, next to Warsaw's 1,000,000 inhabitants) was regarded as the second Polish capital.

Who were these Polish immigrants and why did they settle in America? First, there were the world adventurers; then the artisans brought to America by English colonization agencies; then political refugees, gold seekers, and lastly and in the main part, people fleeing from oppression and hunger, looking for a better life in a new country. Many of the Polish immigrants, through hard work and frugal living, were able to accumulate some savings and soon were in a better financial position than the peasants, laborers, and even intelligentsia in Poland. They were able to send, and still are sending, dollars to Poland for various purposes, among them money for Poland's liberation movements, gifts to relatives, war relief, rebuilding of villages, and help for the churches.

Various Categories

There are Americans of Polish blood with ancestors going back, in some cases, several centuries. Their original names have changed and they live apart from the so-called Polonia which embraces Polish fraternal, social, cultural, political, and religious organizations, identifying themselves, more or less, with the Polish language, customs, and traditions.

In these "Polonia" circles, you'll still find some, but not many, who consider themselves Poles, living only temporarily in America. However, most identify themselves as "Polish-Americans," "American Poles," or Americans of Polish descent or extraction.

A Curious Quasi-government

Since the Second World War, an odd, bizarre, artificial super body imposed itself on this Polish-American sector, called "Polonia," claiming to represent all people of Polish blood in America.

This quasi-government, calling itself the Polish-American Congress, is composed of ambitious officers of large fraternal organizations, which are engaged mostly in selling life insurance and profiting on investing premiums in various mortgages. In addition, it is run by shrewd, cunning politicians, opportunists, and representatives of the bankrupt, so-called Polish government in London.

It resembles the ridiculous governments seen in comic operas. It tries to govern a separate state within a state, an imaginary "Polish-American" nation in the United States.

It's real purpose is to gain personal benefits, political patronage, and fulfillment of high ambitions by displaying a show of Polish Power. I am sure that millions of Americans of Polish descent don't even know of the existence of the Polish-American Congress and are not aware that, without their knowledge or permission, they are being represented by lobbyists in Washington, D.C.

Dual Role Played by Some Leaders

Although many of those posing as Polish-American leaders are American-born, often graduates of American law schools, they pose before the credulous Polish people in America as great Polish patriots, pretending that what they are doing is being done for the good of Poland. There were and are even those who aspire to be leaders, not only of all Polish-Americans, but also of Poles living in other nations and even the Polish nation itself.

In this way they gain confidence and support from the plain, simple people, who would like to do something "for the sake of Poland"; but not for the Poland which exists in reality, not for the Poland which they had to forsake for want of work and bread or freedom and liberty, but for a Poland of their dreams or a Poland of their imagination.

On other convenient occasions, those pretending to be leaders pose as great American patriots and statesmen. They put away the Polish flag and start waving the Star Spangled Banner. Very active in the lower echelons of American political life, they do their utmost to convince the political bosses that they deserve bigger and juicier plums from the patronage yum-yum tree because allegedly millions of Polish votes are under their command.

Not to be accused of being hyphenated Americans, they explain their involvement in Polish organizations on the grounds of a 100 percent American motive: "They are trying to hasten the process of educating and Americanizing the "Polish foreigners."

In reality, however, they are trying to keep the Polish people in America in a ghetto, the access to which would be possible only through them. They keep the fires of their ghetto burning with hate slogans against Americans of other races, national origin, or religious beliefs. Those of Polish descent who mingle with Americans of other nationalities or faiths, or dare to oppose them, are branded as traitors to the Polish cause, heretics, reds, and puppets of the Communists. This contributes to the clannish mentality with which many Polish-Americans are afflicted.

The dual role of "Dr. Jekyll and Mr. Hyde" played by some Polish-American leaders can also be illustrated by the following examples: In Polish communities they claim that only a Roman Catholic can be a good Pole; that Poland must be Roman Catholic or should not exist at all; they condemn the separation of church and state in Poland; they picture the members of Freemasons as devils in human flesh. However, in private and public life among fellow Americans of other nationalities, they express entirely different views. As to religion, they agree that religion is a matter of one's own conscience and they have friends, clients, or customers among Protestants, Jews, freethinkers, and persons without church affiliation; they are not even scared of Masons; on the contrary, they show a great respect for them and even join Masonic lodges.

Not All Leaders Alike

Not all leaders and representatives of the Polish-American world are of the type described above. Certainly there were and are others; honest, able, and educated leaders. Unfortunately, they are in the minority, overshadowed by the mediocre types.

How Strong Are the Organizations Comprising the So-Called Polonia

The pillar of the "Polonia" was the Polish-American press which at one time was comprised of many publications, but now has dwindled to just a few. But there remain some large and influential Polish organizations, formed by the early immigrants. They owe their continued existence to a compulsory life insurance policy requirement for all members and they are the backbone of the "American Polonia."

Describing them as "Polish," I have in mind such organizations which restrict their membership to persons born in Poland or their descendants and relatives in America, including wives or husbands not of Polish descent. Some organizations admit only Roman Catholics who are required, according to the organization's constitution, to prove that they are practicing church members with periodical presentation of certificates, attesting that they went to confession.

The largest and most influential is the Polish National Alliance, abbreviated generally as P.N.A. Officially it has no religious restrictions. The membership, including children and teenagers, was about 340,000 in 1964. It is slowly declining, though reinforced by mergers with smaller fraternal organizations.

The second largest is the Polish Roman-Catholic Union and the third, the Polish Women's Alliance. There are many lesser ones. (Details about organizations in another chapter.)

We may assume that besides the 340,000 in the P.N.A., all other Polish fraternal organizations, basing their strength on the sale of life insurance policies, comprise another 300,000, discounting dual or triple membership. That gives us a membership of 640,000.

How many of them are really active is another thing. There used to be life, discussions and debates in the groups and societies comprising the fraternal organizations, but now the meetings are very poorly attended. Usually the parents send their children to pay the dues and premiums to the financial secretary in order to keep their policies in force—and that's it. Sometimes a special inducement like free beer and lunch, or a card game after the meeting brings a larger crowd.

Other Polish Organizations

Besides the fraternal organizations with their fairly well-paid officers and large staffs of employees, the "American Polonia" includes organizations of a different nature, such as:

theatrical groups, singing and dancing societies and other cultural clubs, Polish veterans of various wars, armies, and commands. Most of these club or society members belong to one or more fraternal organizations.

Now let us see what the count is in other Polish-American sectors.

Post World War II Immigration

These newest Polish immigrants, comprised mainly of people called formerly "Displaced Persons" and brought to America thanks to the sponsorship of various organizations and private persons form another Polish-American sector—very much in contrast with the old immigration.

The old immigrants came here mostly as plain, hardworking, poorly educated people. The new immigrants are on a higher educational level and more sophisticated, having gone through various life experiences. Many of them, being sponsored, obtained employment without difficulty and didn't have to start the hard way, from the bottom of the ladder, as their predecessors.

The least numerous but the loudest among them are the old style Polish intelligentsia, characterized by the known saying, "Where there are 100 Poles, there are ninety-nine parties or cliques." Among them are many disgruntled, frustrated, hate-mongering, and revengeful people. They like to be looked upon as Polish patriots-conspirators and they have formed various groups, getting their inspiration from leaders of various cliques of frustrated Polish gentry in London, Paris, Madrid, and Rome. The Polish American Congress gets strong support from them because they like the idea of a separate Polish state within a state, and they count on moral and financial support for their causes from this congress.

There are also others, trying to make good in America and to forget their experiences in Nazi labor or concentration camps, or life in exile or suffering in Poland. Among them are many university graduates and professionals; engineers, jurists, chemists, artists, writers, and poets. There are also craftsmen, skilled and unskilled workers, soldiers, officers and members of the Polish army, navy, merchant marine, and air force who served under British command during World War II. This sector of Polish immigrants in America (by the expression "America" I mean mostly in the U.S.A., although it applies also to the situation in Canada) has its own clubs, societies, and organizations—which are usually closed to other Polish-Americans. Some of them, however, joined the organizations of the "Polonia" world; others don't belong to any strictly Polish organizations. Their number, together with those Polish people who were lucky to come here, under existing laws and quotas, directly from Poland after World War II, may be counted in hundreds of thousands.

The Most Numerous Polish-American World

It is not the "Polonia" with its societies and large fraternal organizations, it is not the post-World War II immigration; the most numerous are the Americans of Polish blood who came here as children or were born in America from Polish or partly Polish parents and their descendants.

While the rapidly diminishing Polish-language press is like a mirror of events in the two previously mentioned worlds—the English-language American press is a mirror of the third Polish-American world.

Let's look closely at any of the metropolitan dailies, published in such cities as Chicago, New York, Detroit, Milwaukee, Buffalo, Cleveland, Toledo, Boston, or Pittsburgh. The general news is full of Polish-sounding names; nearly on every page, in every sector of American life. On the first page, in reports from the federal capital, Washington, Polish names of U.S. congressmen and government officials are part of the news.

Names Don't Reveal Everything

You can't judge solely by the name whether a person is of Polish descent or not. It may be that there are more Polish-Americans and people of Polish descent without than with a Polish-sounding name. That doesn't mean that they have changed their names. There are many Americans of Polish descent with German-sounding names, including myself. How come? Sometimes their forefathers were Germans who settled in Poland, married Polish women, and their offspring became Polish by assimilation. On the other hand, many Polish names were changed under pressure or forcefully or "by mistake" in a birth certificate during the period of time when Poland was under German rule.

There are some Polish-Americans who changed their names for other reasons. In feudal Poland, it often happened that the landlord-squire or nobleman gave his subject, the peasant, an insulting, derogative, or ridiculous name, which then was transferred from father to son.

Others were compelled to change their Polish names, often very difficult to pronounce, for business, family, or other reasons or conditions of life. Usually they shortened their name or gave them the English equivalent.

"Polonized" Americans of Various Descents

There are many cases where a man or a woman will marry a Polish-American and live closely with his or her Polish parents or grandparents or other members of the Polish family. As a result they get accustomed to Polish traditions, Polish ways of cooking, and even learn certain Polish expressions. And so do their children.

In Chicago, and Detroit's Polish suburb, Hamtramck, I met several Negroes who could speak Polish fairly well. I even knew of an American Negro among the American volunteers in the Polish Army in France during World War I.

There are many Polish-Americans, especially small businessmen who are known popularly as "Casey," "Murphy," etc. People deal with them unaware that they are Polish, because they use their Polish family name usually only when signing documents.

This process of changed names can be understood by reading death notices in newspapers of cities with a large Polish-American population.

For example: Let's suppose that a death notice pertains to a man with the Polish name of "Trojanowski" or "Zielinski." We may read that he left several sons, some of them having changed their name to "Troy" or "Green." (The name Zielinski implies a green color). The names of his surviving married daughters may denote the various nationalities of their husbands; such as Schmidt, McCarthy, Piccolini, Hanson, De-Latour, and so on. Then there may be a mention about relatives surviving in Poland and you may assume that there was something binding, more or less, not only the dead man, but also Mr. Troy, Mr. Green, Mrs. Schmidt, Mrs. McCarthy, Mrs. Piccolini, Mrs. Hanson, or Mrs. DeLatour with Polish people not only here in America, but in Poland as well.

On the other hand, let's suppose there is a death notice pertaining to a non-Polish name like "Grudy," "Bartz" or "Rusk." Among the surviving relatives, we may find Polish names like Grudzielanek or Grudkowski, Barczak or Barczynski, Ruszczak or Ruszkiewicz. And again, we find that the name "Grudy," "Bartz" or "Rusk" was changed from one of the abovementioned Polish names.

So, in the future, if you meet a person with a German, Irish, Italian, French, or Scandinavian-sounding name, don't be too sure that there is not some Polish blood in him or her. On the contrary, if you meet a person with a Polish name, don't take for granted that he or she is Polish.

Diversity Among the Third Polish-American World

People belonging more or less to this third Polish-American world can be found, as I mentioned before, in almost every sector of American life. For example:

In the American executive government—former Postmaster General Gronouski, and in 1977, the President's National Security Adviser—Zbigniew Brzezinski.

There are Polish-Americans:

In the legislative branch of the government as representatives in the United States Congress and in various governmental departments and agencies.

As state senators and assemblymen, county and city officials, and most numerous as policemen, firemen, county, and city workers.

Among professions as scholars, college professors, instructors, teachers, doctors, dentists, lawyers, engineers, etc.

In the field of sports, where many Polish-Americans achieved their stardom.

In the financial, business, commerce, and industry field; among bankers, merchants, industrialists (although very few can be classified as millionaires). The small business field seems to be the specialty of Polish-Americans.

Some, but relatively not too many, among the leaders of organized labor.

The great majority, however, consists of skilled and unskilled factory workers in cities and farmers in rural areas.

Towns and Cities With Polish Names

Many American towns and cities have historic Polish names, like: Krakow or Cracow, Warsaw, Lublin, Kosciusko, Pulaski, Poland, and Panna Marya. Most of them were so named by the first Polish settlers. Some of them had hardly any Polish population, but were given a Polish name to honor certain Poles or certain Polish achievements.

There are other "Polish" towns and cities in America

considered as Polish because most of the inhabitants are of Polish descent, although the name of the city is not Polish; one of such formerly strictly Polish cities, now gradually losing its original character, is Hamtramck, Michigan.

There are, however, still many sectors of American life where Americans of Polish descent are unable to gain access, partly because of discrimination, partly because they still lack certain qualifications.

As an example of how an American of Polish descent and Polish name may be discriminated against, although one has the highest education and best qualifications, is the case of former Postmaster General Gronouski. When his nomination by the late President Kennedy was made public, some circles were aroused with criticism that his name ended with the Polish ''ski.'' It seems that the criticism and opposition to President Kennedy's nomination of Mr. Gronouski as Postmaster General was based on prejudice against Polish names and Polish descent and the fear that President Kennedy would gain support in the election by showing that he is not discriminating against Americans of Polish descent.

Great Changes

Mr. Gronouski is not the first Polish-American who won a high post in Washington without being a protégé of Polish-American politicians. So is Zbigniew Brzezinski and Senator Muskie from Maine, one-time potential candidate for president of the United States.

Among several others, whose names cling in my memory, is the name of Congressman Zajacek from the state of Washington. A son of a hard-working Polish woman, without any substantial Polish-American vote or support, he became one of the most capable young United States Congressmen. Too bad his life ended prematurely due to a tragic death, caused, no doubt, by strain of overwork.

The maxim of delivering the Polish vote, boxed, packaged, and sealed, is outdated. The times are gone when a priest could influence and a saloonkeeper could deliver the votes. The differences in religion and nationality are not such a deciding factor in this third Polish-American world as they are in the two other worlds.

The city of Milwaukee can serve as a good example. For a long time, the office of the mayor of Milwaukee was in the hands of Mr. Zeidler, of German descent, of Protestant religion, and of the Socialist party. In each election, however, he won, thanks to the support given him in the wards inhabited predominantly by citizens of Polish extraction. The reason? Because he was regarded as an honest man, without the stigma of a "crooked politician" and he did not discriminate against Americans of Polish descent.

How Big Is the Polish-American World?

It all depends on who counts and how the counting is done. For instance, as I've mentioned before, some Polish-American leaders and politicians repeat for decades, parrot-like, without trying to do any research, that they are representing a world consisting of seven million Polish-Americans.

Those who dislike Polish-Americans are more liberal in the process of counting. They can nose out a "Pollack" everywhere and according to them, every third or fourth American is nothing but a "Pollack."

I also remember the horrified exclamations of the one-time renowned Father Coughlin, a Roman Catholic priest, politician, and radio personality, who was afraid that "if things will go on like that, instead of Washington, we'll have Washingtonski." So far, however, the barbaric hordes of Polish-Americans have not overrun the American capitol and it's still Washington and not Washingtonski.

According to my estimate, the number of people in the United States with more or less Polish blood in their veins, is over fifteen million.

III

What Binds and What Separates People of Polish Blood

The old, traditional saying that "Polish-Americans are unified by religion and language of their forefathers" is not quite true.

In many cases it is religion, dialects, derivation from regions formerly under Russian, Austrian, or German rule, inherited traditions and beliefs that cause a division among them.

There is one common denominator for all Poles living in America, be it Polish-Americans or Americans of Polish descent, namely: "Polish Blood."

What is the Definition of "Polish Blood"

Polish blood reveals itself by the peculiarities that mark the Polish character, with its good and bad qualities, customs and habits.

It is usually manifested on the one side by such traits as a strong temperament, enormous courage, bordering often on foolhardiness or contempt of life, great endurance, permitting one to bear one's fate or suffering with patience, natural talents, especially in the fields of music, dance, and song. On the other side, great sentimentality, sincerity stretched sometimes to naivete, sense of loyalty, humbleness, and submissiveness to things or persons regarded as saintly or superior.

One may say that the Polish character is as diversified and changeable as the world-known music of the famous Polish composer, Chopin, whose romantic melodies, especially mazurkas and polonaises symbolize the traits of Polish blood.

Another description of Polish blood is a Polish proverb, saying that a Pole is good for drinking and fighting. As drinkers, they have gained a somewhat unflattering reputation, similar to that held by the Irishmen. Their hard and troubled life and other conditions have a lot to do with it. As fighters, they are considered among the best. As a student at the officer candidate school at Ft. Benning, Ga., upon the discovery that I am Polish, I was told by a high-ranking member of the infantry school command: "Some of the best soldiers in the United States Army are Polish and we are proud of them. Every company in our army has at least one first-class Polish soldier."

The Polish Stomach

Polish blood may also be detected by the way of the stomach; the eating habits and customs prevailing most conspicuously during such holidays as Christmas and Easter.

I do not mean to imply that the eating habits of the more prosperous people of Poland are preserved here in America. According to the glorified old Polish custom (excluding the poor classes) a Polish meal during festive occasions consisted of about twelve courses, plus additional side dishes and enormous quantities of beverages, mostly alcoholic.

However, the Polish way of eating is preserved here in the more simple foods like kielbasa (Polish sausage), kishka (blood-barley sausage), and a variety of other sausages. Then there are all kinds of "pierogi" (somewhat similar to ravioli) filled with meat, cheese, mashed potatoes, kraut, or berries. Another dish is "kluski" (a type of dumpling) usually filled with plums. Soups are an important part of the Polish diet, some typical ones are: barszcz (borsht), czarnina (blood soup), and flaczki (tripe soup). Among Polish pastries are babki, paczki, chrust, and many kinds of tortes.

In general, Polish-style food is like cement, binding people of Polish blood.

Antagonisms Among Immigrants Influenced Their Children in America

The greatest influx of Polish immigrants to America was at the end of the nineteenth and beginning of the twentieth century during which time Poland was occupied by Russia, Germany, and Austria.

The policy of the occupation powers, based on the Roman conquerors' principle: "Divide et impera," (divide and rule), was very successful and left its stigma to this day upon the Polish people in America and their descendants. Taught by these powers to hate each other, the immigrants settled in separate, antagonistic groups and called each other insulting names such as "Rusek" (one from the Russian occupation), "Prusek" (one from the Prussian occuaption), or "Galon" (one from Little Poland, known as "Galicia" under Austrian occupation).

Let me give you a vivid example of these conditions, as I observed them as a youngster in Toledo, Ohio, in about 1916. I had a very good and busy observation post, being from early morning until noon a reporter for a Polish-American newspaper; in the afternonon a sort of investigator for the Toledo Board of Education, taking a census of children of school age in Polish neighborhoods; in the evening a member of a small Polish theatrical stock company. One part of the city, inhabited mostly by Poles who came from the German occupation was given by other Toledo Poles the insulting German name, "Kuhschwantz," translated literally, "a cow's tail;" the Polish settlement on the opposite side of the city, inhabited by Poles from Russian-occupied Poland, was called in turn "szew-cowo," translated literally, "a cobblers' patch." In Polish, the term "cobbler" when applied generally, had a derogatory meaning.

The children of these Polish settlers, born here in free America, inherited this antagonism. It manifested itself sometimes in beating up a boy from one Polish neighborhood who dared to go out with a girl from a different Polish neighborhood; in brawls at Polish weddings, etc.

These differences and divisions still exist, not only in Toledo, Ohio, but in many of the densely populated Polish neighborhoods of major American cities. Fortunately, they are becoming less acute.

Antagonisms Based on Status and Language

The social strata from which the Polish immigrants originated, and the language they used in common conversation, are responsible for additional divisions among the Polish people in America.

The most numerous immigrants were the peasants, and they were of all sorts; some unable to read and write; some possessing more or less schooling and experience. They came from different parts of Poland, speaking different dialects—this segregated them into clannish groups, distrustful of one another. Among them were the mountaineers from the Carpathian mountains in southern Poland and fishermen from the Baltic region of northern Poland.

Then there were townsmen, professionals, craftsmen, more or less skilled factory workers, and students with unfinished higher education. These spoke grammatical Polish, regarded themselves as "intelligentsia," and didn't mingle with the dialect-speaking immigrants unless they were forced to do so by conditions beyond their control, by an opportunity for a good business transaction, or by a desire to lift their fellow countrymen to a higher level.

21

Another class of Polish immigrants, who aspired to be somewhat better than the others, were those claiming to be of the Polish "szlachta" (gentry, squires, and nobility).

However, all of them were alike in looking for the American dollar. These divisions are now less significant, but they still exist in somewhat changed forms.

Antagonisms Based on Religious Beliefs

Most of the Polish immigrants were very devout Roman Catholics, but their religious beliefs, customs, and prayers were different from other Roman Catholics in America. Their religion was combined with Polish patriotism, old Polish customs and traditions, dating back to the pre-Christian era.

For example, they had their own Polish saints, who played an important part in Poland's history, such as St. Stanislaus, St. Casimir, St. Hedwig, and many others.

Saint Mary, regarded by all Roman Catholics as the Blessed Virgin Mary, was hailed in prayers as the Queen of the Polish Crown and there were several different portrayals of her and her role in the Polish nation as shown at the three best-known shrines in Poland: one in Czestochowa, one in Ostrobrama, one in Zebrzydow, and at several lesser-known ones.

Jesus Christ was also regarded as a symbol of Poland's martyrdom. Christmas and Easter, besides their religious meaning, had an additional character as Polish national holidays, symbolizing renunification, rejuvenation, and rebirth of the Polish nation.

Besides the Roman Catholics, there were some Protestants, Jews, members of the Orthodox church, and of other religious groups, and also those not affiliated with any religious group.

Effects of American Freedom

In Poland the affiliation with the Roman Catholic church

was a necessity. In that part of Poland under Austrian rule, the Roman Catholic religion was the state religion. In other parts of partitioned Poland, it was the bond that kept the Polish people together, helpful in resisting oppression and schemes to exterminate the Polish race. (There were some exceptions to this. There were cases where the Roman Catholic church was used by some German bishops as an instrument to germanize the Polish people). As far as the Polish peasant was concerned—to disobey a priest in or out of the church was tantamount to heresy and resulted in exclusion from society.

After the Polish immigrants tasted the formerly forbidden fruit from the American freedom tree—after realizing that they were living in a country based on separation of church and state, after attending various meetings, listening to various discussions and speeches or reading formerly forbidden literature—most of their newly founded Polish Roman Catholic parishes underwent a series of more or less radical uprisings and changes—resulting eventually in the establishment of new Polish religious groups—or in Polish people joining other churches or sects, or in complete disassociation from the church.

The most common grievances of Polish-Americans at that time were:

a. The autocratic behavior of some Catholic priests or their housekeepers.
b. Lack of financial accounting from collections and general parish finances.
c. The signing over of the parish property to the bishop, who usually was of German or Irish nationality and, therefore, was regarded as hostile to the Polish people, treating them as secondary Catholics.
d. The greatest grievance, and it exists to this day, is that the numerous Polish Roman Catholics are not given proper representation in the church hierarchy.

This last grievance resulted among others in the establishment of the Polish National Catholic Church in America, totally independent of the Vatican.

Clergymen Lose Their Absolute Control

Another cause of friction, which lasted for a quite a long time but subsided in the pre-World War II era, was the movement to organize independent Polish clubs and societies outside the Polish parishes, beyond the control of clergymen.

Those who dared to break away from the absolute clerical control were viciously condemned from the pulpit and by the press, controlled by the priests. In turn, organizers of Polish independent societies began to publish their own independent Polish newspapers, criticizing the behavior of the Polish Roman Catholic clergymen and conditions existing in the parishes.

Some of the independent Polish newspapers were put on index (a listing of publications forbidden by the Church). In some churches the people would be asked at confession if they read certain independent Polish newspapers and if they admitted it, they were refused absolution. Newsboys, delivering independent newspapers, were reprimanded or even terrorized by priests.

Nevertheless, the independent Polish-American newspapers grew in circulation and the independent Polish organizations grew in membership. Among others, the Polish National Alliance, today the largest Polish-American organization, went through this process of clerical persecution.

Pertaining to Polish-American organizations, independent of the Roman-Catholic church, very little is known nowadays of the movement to organize Polish-American Freemasonry lodges. To document their existence I have a reproduction of a diploma, issued to my father, Franciszek Friedel, in 1918 in Toledo, Ohio. The organizer of this particular Polish-American lodge was A. A. Paryski, publisher and editor of Toldeo's Polish daily and weekly newspaper, *Ameryka-Echo*.

There was a segment of more liberal and broad-minded Polish-American clergy, which did not take part in this persecution; there were even Polish Roman Catholic priests who openly sided with the rebellion against clerical autocracy.

In due time this friction recessed and more and more clergymen started joining the ever-growing independent Polish organizations. As a result of this change of tactics, although the Polish-American clergy lost its absolute control, it did not lose its great influence in Polish-American communities.

The independent Polish newspapers and organizations were not the only critics of the Polish-American clergy. The most humiliating blow was delivered in the late thirties by Cardinal Mundelein, the Archbishop of Chicago, in his memorial to the Holy See, in which he condemned the behavior and morals of the Polish-American clergy in very strong terms. Cardinal Mundelein's memorial, humiliating the Polish-American clergy, created at that time a great furor among Polish-American clergymen. Some of the accused voiced the opinion that Cardinal Mundelein did it to offset their demands for equal treatment and elevation of Polish-American priests to higher posts, and in revenge because of complaints made by them to the Pope about bias and unfair treatment of Polish-American clergy by the German and Irish-American hierarchy.

What Binds Polish-Americans?

Now conditions have changed somewhat for the better. But the paramount question remains: Why this discrimination, why the unfair treatment? And, truly, this question is the greatest factor that binds solidly all Polish-Americans, no matter what religion, what generation, or what other differences are between them. As long as Polish-Americans feel that they are being treated as second-class citizens, that they are victims of bias and prejudice because of their nationality, they'll stick together as one group.

Dissent Among the Polish-American Clergy

As a journalist, I remember that even the Polish Roman Catholic clergy in America was divided into various camps, antagonistic to each other. For example: There were priests belonging to different orders, jealous of each other. The most important among them were the Polish Resurrectionists (a branch of the Jesuits) and the Polish Franciscans. The Franciscans themselves were divided into two groups, called in Polish-American circles "the brown ones" and "the black ones," with strong animosities and rivalries between them. In the other camp, with different viewpoints, angles, and interests were the secular priests.

Among the first Polish clergymen in America were some of those who gained everlasting popularity, friendship, and respect among the Polish immigrants because they helped them get accustomed to new conditions of life and worked and suffered together with them.

But there were also others who cared mostly about their own comfort and welfare, who didn't co-operate with their people. Instead of acting as shepherds, solicitous of their herd, they were more interested in shearing the sheeps' wool.

There also were courageous clergymen, many of them Polish patriots. They earned the displeasure of their superiors who were opposed to mixing religion with Polish patriotism, opposed to the teaching of the Polish language in the church schools or making collections for strictly Polish charitable or patriotic causes in the church or on the church grounds.

On the other side, there were those who tried to gain the confidence and favors of superiors by their obvious efforts to abolish the Polish character of the parishes and supplant the names of Polish Roman Catholic saints given some churches by the original founders, with names of non-Polish Roman Catholic saints. For example, "St. Stanislaus" school or church was changed to "Notre Dame" and so on.

Treatment of Poles of Another Religion

The internal friction in the Polish Roman Catholic communities was nothing compared to the treatment Polish people of other religions were accorded by Roman Catholic zealots. Many Polish Protestants and Jews were compelled to withdraw from Polish organizational life to avoid daily humiliations and provocations. They joined with Americans of other nationalities who professed a similar faith. These individuals received the worst treatment. Very often they had to move out of Polish neighborhoods, being called such names as: infidels, unbelievers, devils, heretics, radicals, and reds.

New, small congregations began to appear, organized by Polish Baptists, Polish Bible students, Old Catholics, Independent Catholics, and similar sects. A great number of dissidents organized or joined a new church, The Polish National Catholic Church, which grew, according to pre-World War II estimates into a religious organization embracing several hundred thousand members.

This religious breach did not end in name calling. The children of Polish people, belonging to the new church were often spat upon or stoned by children of Polish Roman Catholics, provoked by their fanatic parents or priests and nuns.

There were brawls, street fighting, and even shooting and killing. In Pennsylvania, the cradle of the Polish National Catholic Church movement, there are cemeteries with graves and monuments, testifying to Polish-American victims of religious fanaticism. Fortunately, this barbaric form of settling religious differences has now ceased.

It is an irony that one of the tenets, which caused the tragic schism in the Polish Roman Catholic camp, namely, the use of the native tongue instead of Latin, has now been accepted as one of the principal reforms of the Roman Catholic church in America.

Antagonisms Based on Politics

Politics are always a cause of friction. As far as Polish-Americans are concerned, divisions were and still are caused not only by domestic political differences, but also by the political situation in Poland.

Animosity Toward Poles of Jewish Origin

It is characteristic that people who complain of persecution and prejudice like to persecute others. For some time, in the circles of the Polish-American intelligentsia, which were and are very small in relation to the masses of Polish working people, some of the most energetic, progressive, and enterprising were Poles of Jewish origin. What happened to them is a sad commentary on Polish-American life. Most of them could not stand the hostile attitude, ridicule, and sneering, shown them by less talented or bigoted countrymen.

Disgusted and frustrated, they began to drift away from the Polish-American communities and activities. Some tried to erase the traces of their Jewish descent by accepting the Roman Catholic religion. Nevertheless, ill will was shown against them on every occasion. In the Polish-American press and during controversies at meetings, they were pointed out critically as neophytes or converted Jews.

The masses of Polish-American working people had and still have paradoxically two contrary attitudes toward Jews in general. On the one side, ridicule or contempt; on the other side, respect and confidence. In everyday conversations, they like to make jokes about Jews or use stereotyped contemptuous phrases. But when they need something, be it merchandise, financial, medical, or legal help, many of them prefer to go to a Jew than to their own countryman. There is an old Polish proverb for this attitude: "Jak bieda, to do Zyda." (When in need, go to a Jew.)

Bitterness Toward the Upper Class

Since the end of the nineteenth century, when Polish immigrants began to arrive here in larger numbers, they were being exploited mercilessly by some of their own countrymen from the upper classes, who came to this country before them and offered themselves as guides, advisors, and leaders.

The result is distrust, bitterness, and division among Polish-Americans. As a vivid illustration of how newcomers were exploited, here is an excerpt translated from the book *Notatki z Podrozy* (Notes From My Journey) written by S. Nesterowicz and published in 1910 by the A. A. Paryski Publishing Company of Toledo, Ohio:

As a result of letters we've received from our countryman, living in America, telling us what a good life we can have on his large farm, we decided to take advantage of his offer.

Altogether, 48 families made the long, burdensome trip from Poland to America. In the Spring of 1874 we arrived in Cretendon, Arkansas, where our countryman, together with another man, had a 1,600-acre cotton plantation.

We were given some dilapidated shanties for our housing and we were told that according to the law of the land we were now his slaves and that the penalty for desertion was death. Each family was given four pounds of wheat flour and four pounds of corn flour, without anything additional. This was supposed to last us for one week. Besides us men, our wives and all children over five years of age had to work in the fields. We were promised eight dollars a month for each family but the money could be taken out only in merchandise.

God knows what would have happened to us were it not for a Jewish peddler, who visited the plantation and explained to us that there is no slavery in America and we can't be punished by death for leaving the plantation.

When the occasion arose, we ran away to Memphis, leaving most of our belongings behind.

The plantation owner came there after us, but the Jewish people gave us protection. They found work for us men and the Order of German Franciscan Fathers took care of our families.

The most common trap in those times, besides enlisting Polish people deceptively as a working force, was the swindle under the guise of establishing Polish farm colonies. Enticed by the beautiful description of the land and trusting their eloquent countrymen, Polish people would spend their hard-earned money to buy the promised land, only to find out upon their arrival at the destination that the land was not fit for cultivation.

Using Polish Patriotism as a Bait

Numerous other schemes were perpetrated upon the credulous Polish people, in the golden era following World War I, by some members of the so-called Polish intelligentsia.

This was the era of selling shares for newly founded corporations, which were to be established in resurrected Poland. These corporations kept springing up like mushrooms after a rain. It was also a period of organizing business firms in America with Polish-American management and Polish-American workers. The share-selling activities were conducted under such patriotic slogans as: "Help Build the Polish Industry!"; "Help in Establishing a Great Polish Merchant Marine!"; or, "Let's Build Up Polish-American Commerce!" Most of these firms went out of existence as soon as the sale of shares ceased. Many prominent Polish-American leaders and newspapers were used as tools or participated knowingly in these easy but dishonest money-making schemes.

Taking Advantage of Ignorance

There were some Polish-American leaders who tried their best to educate their countrymen and raise them to higher levels. But, there were also others who made a handsome profit on the ignorance of the Polish people. The selling of miraculous medicines and all kinds of rackets revolving around fortune-telling were the most common methods of fleecing the ignorant and superstitious.

As an illustration of how this was done, I am relating my own experience as a part-time clerk in a Polish drug store in Chicago during the years preceding World War I.

The drug store specialized in medicines and salves, which some Polish people regarded as miraculous. Among others, there was "mosquito lard" and "bear's lard" for sale. Whenever customers asked for mosquito lard, I was instructed by the pharmacist, one of Chicago's great Polish leaders, to sell them a miniature container, filled with plain cold cream, naturally at a high price. Bear's lard was sold in larger containers, also filled with cold cream, but at a lower price.

Time and again, Polish men or women would come to the pharmacist, seeking medical advice, thinking, in their cunning way, that this way it would be cheaper and better for them. In the first place, they wouldn't have to pay a doctor or go through all the trouble of waiting and undressing; secondly, the pharmacist had such a variety of medicines that he would be able to give them a better choice than the doctor.

The pharmacist would take them to a corner and start inquiries about their ailments. For each ailment he would give them a bottle or box of medicine, guaranteeing good results but under one condition: "While taking this medicine, you can't touch whiskey, wine or even beer; otherwise all the medicine is for nothing."

Some weeks later the same man or woman would appear with loud complaints. They had paid so much for the miraculous medicine and it didn't help them at all, in fact the ailment had gotten worse. The pharmacist would listen to their complaints in patience. After they were through he would start asking questions: "Now, are you sure, you didn't have something to drink? Just think hard and don't lie to me." Naturally, it came out during the shrewd interrogation that they had something to drink. Maybe it was at a christening or funeral or wedding, and as good Poles they just couldn't refuse a drink.

Then the pharmacist started his "spiel" of offended dignity. "A man of science gives you remedies that can't fail, gives you everything he has learned in schools in an arduous, expensive way, and you are trying to take advantage of him, to deceive him! You should be ashamed of yourself." The result was that the man or woman apologized humbly to "mister pharmacist" and bought some more of his miraculous medicine.

I didn't last very long in this drug store, having committed a crime against this sort of Polish leadership. I was caught in the process of trying to explain to a woman that there is no such thing as mosquito lard.

The Era of Great Despair

During the great economic depression, preceding World War II, many Polish-Americans lost their money, savings, and property. They blamed the merchants, lawyers, doctors, real estate men, and directors of small Polish-American banks and savings and loan associations for their losses. This again caused distrust of the upper class and disunity among people of Polish extraction. Surely, the depression left an impact on the whole American nation, but the Polish-American segment was hit the hardest and very often through the dishonesty or lack of qualifications of its leaders.

At that time a powerful, warning voice came from a representative of the more liberal American-born Roman Catholic clergy of Polish nationality. The Rt. Rev. Stephen Woznicki, nominated auxiliary bishop-elect of Detroit, Michigan, on December 11, 1937, criticized vigorously the behavior of the Polish-American upper class and blamed their conduct for creating distrust and disunity.

With the outbreak of World War II and the German invasion of Poland, came a wave unifying somewhat all Polish-Americans, regardless, of where they were born or from what

32

generation. When Warsaw fell, there were tears in the eyes and lumps in the throats of many Polish-Americans. Even those who were far removed from the Polish-American mainstream, felt instinctively what the future was holding for an American with the slightest trace of Polish blood or Polish relationship should the Nazi policy of hate, genocide, and extermination of Polish people be successful.

Post-War II Divisions Among Polish-Americans

The causes, responsible for differences, divisions, and disunity in this era are similar to those dividing the whole American society. Paramount are the following divisions:

First is the division between those Polish people who still stick to the old ways and traditions and the Polish people who think young, are more broadminded, look more to the future than to the past and are disengaged from the currents of clannish hate and quarrels. This is not necessarily a division between young and old as far as age is concerned; or between those born in Poland or America. Sometimes the American-born stick more to old country traditions, superstitions, and behavior than those born in Poland.

This division was evident especially in the large Polish-American organizations where the old cliques held, with all possible cunning and tricks, onto their elective governing positions and wouldn't let the younger element get into the driver's seat. Let's take for example the largest Polish-American organization, the Polish National Alliance. An all-powerful president of this organization was elected at the convention held in September 1963 in Philadelphia, Pa. for the seventh time in a row. Since elective conventions are held every four years, it means that the same man and his cronies held power consecutively for over a quarter of a century. The opposition to such a long rule by one man and his clique was squashed at the convention by a very shrewd method. Here's how it was done.

The proposal to limit the term of elective officeholders to

two four-year tenures was put to a vote not by a secret ballot of delegates, but by raising of hands. In this way the president and his cronies could see who is for them and who is against and as a result, the proposal was voted down. The old rulers remained in the driver's seats and there wasn't much chance of young blood, fresh minds, and new ideas rejuvenating the organization.

Unfriendliness Toward D.P.'s

The second division is between post-World War II Polish immigrants, classified usually as Displaced Persons, and the old settlers or American-born Polish people.

One of the main reasons is that these two Polish groups simply do not understand each other.

Most disliked among Polish-Americans are some D.P.'s of the old-style Polish gentry who simply can't go along with the American way of life, but would like to transplant to this country the old European caste system.

Division Created by American Social Reform Movements

The third and most recent division among Polish-Americans is caused by social problems and crusades for reforms.

It is a pity that there are so few Polish-American leaders interested in American crusades for social reforms . . . and yet the Polish nationality should be synonymous with the revolutionary slogans: "For freedom, liberty, equality!"

In most American cities many Polish-American leaders have shown a very hostile attitude toward the Negro freedom movement, equating it with lawless acts, committed by Negro groups, gangs, or individuals.

And yet the great Polish-American, of whom they all are

so proud and whose name they mention every time they want to be recognized as equal American citizens, Gen. Thaddeus Kosciuszko, gave them a better example.

He not only fought for American independence, but also supported the principle of political equality among men. He urged that the Negro slaves in America be freed and educated. He himself emancipated not only the Polish serfs from the slavery of the Polish feudal system, but also the Negroes on the estates given him by the United States government. According to Kosciuszko's last will, 500 acres of public land and restitution of $15,000 for his personal expenses, granted him by the U.S. Congress, were to be spent for the good of Negroes. His legacy established the first school for Negroes, founded in Newark, New Jersey.

And were Gen. Thaddeus Kosciuszko today among our Polish-Americans, he would, no doubt, lead Americans of Polish ancestry in a movement supporting human rights for Negroes.

There is, however, a very important and understandable reason why Polish-Americans in the majority are antagonistic and afraid of Negroes, especially in such cities as Detroit, Michigan.

Some of them were victimized by holdups, burglaries, robberies, and other violent acts committed by gangs of Negroes. Due to the influx of Negroes into Polish neighborhoods, their properties lost value. Many panicked and moved out, selling their houses at a big loss. And many others are frightened that along with equal rights given the Negroes the following may happen to them:

1. That their children may marry Negroes.
2. That their property may lose its value if Negroes will have housing equality.
3. That someone in their family may lose their job if Negroes are given equal employment opportunities.

Most Polish-American leaders prey on these fears and apprehensions and although they know better, they don't do anything to explain the Negro freedom movement and separate it from the lawlessness, vandalism, and terrorism committed by many Negroes under the guise of the freedom movement.

However, there were and are some Polish-Americans brave enough to be martyred or stoned by their countrymen, expressing sympathy for the American Negroes or Blacks as they prefer to be called now. Here are some examples:

The young breed of future Polish-American priests, studying at the Roman Catholic Polish Theological Seminary in Orchard Lake, Michigan, published some time ago in their monthly magazine *Sodalis* an article supporting the "Negro revolution" and stating reasons why all Polish-Americans should support the Negro cause.

Some Polish Roman Catholic priests in Milwaukee and several other cities, had the courage, notwithstanding the indignation and even ire of their parishioners, to call from the pulpit for the support and understanding of the aims of the Negro freedom movement. I'll mention especially one, who, as I was told by some of his parishioners, was very frank and courageous in this matter; namely, the pastor of SS. Cyril and Methodius Church, Father Alphonse Popek, former professor at St. Francis Seminary. This church is one of the oldest and largest Polish congregations in Milwaukee, located in the heart of the Polish community.

And again, looking through the *Milwaukee Sentinel* (issue of November 11, 1963) in "Letters to the Editor," I read about the activities of "Project Friendship," an organization sponsoring mutual visits and discussions among people of the Negro and white races. And who signed as the head of this organization? Robert J. Czajkowski.

Another opinion was voiced at a convention of Polish-American Cultural Clubs, held in Milwaukee in August of 1963. In a memorial, sent to President Kennedy and published in the "Polish Daily News" in Chicago (Dziennik Chicagoski) on August 15, 1963, the opinion was voiced that goals for betterment should not be achieved by lawlessness or special class legislation.

The pro and con attitudes pertaining to the support of Negro rights and other social problems are going to divide Polish-American people into antagonistic groups for a long time to come.

Polish-Americans and Present Poland

Most Polish-Americans are fully aware of the discrimination practiced against their nationality and are trying to offset it by showing that they are good, loyal Americans.

Therefore, some are even afraid to mention Poland, since it is now in the sphere of Soviet influence.

Others realize that existing conditions are necessary for Poland's survival. Its people had barely escaped complete extermination, as planned by the Nazi German government, and similar plans are still in the minds of some German elements and one never knows when these elements will take over.

However, every year more and more group excursions and private trips by plane or ship are being made to Poland, not only to visit relatives, but also by people of Polish blood without any known relatives in Poland. Their purpose: To see the country and places from where their forefathers came and to see the historic sites, culture, landscapes, people, and the way of life in present Poland. Even Roman-Catholic priests and nuns take part in these excursions or trips.

IV

The Polish-American Conversational Language

Grammatical Polish language is used in small, restricted circles, but seldom in the majority of Polish-American homes.

For conversation among themselves and in their community stores, owned by their fellow-countrymen, a unique Polish-American jargon is used, composed of polonized English words and American expressions.

This conversational language is not written; it is only spoken. It comes directly out of the life of its people. The people using this language may be compared to street musicians playing tunes without knowing how to read or write music.

How Did This Language Originate?

Many of the Polish people who came to America a long time ago could barely read or write, but they had good ears. They memorized the English sounds, changed them a little and thus new words were born.

There were others who could read and write, but they found here, in America, certain conditions, products, inventions, gadgets, tools, and customs unknown to them in the country from which they came and difficult to describe in the Polish vocabulary they knew.

Their children learned the new words and expressions and used them at home and in conversation with their friends and neighbors, and sometimes even improvised on them. Their children, the third generation, did likewise and presto—the peculiar Polish-American jargon was born.

This jargon is very flexible and undergoes constant changes. It may be a little different in Chicago than it is in Milwaukee or Buffalo or Detroit or Cleveland. It even differs in various parts of the same city, depending upon the Polish dialect prevalent in the particular Polish neighborhood.

This Polish-American jargon has a long history in the United States; it has been used for over one hundred years.

Polish-American salesmen, insurance agents, and businessmen knew the value of this jargon. By using it instead of English or good Polish, they could approach their customers or clients on a more intimate footing, which ultimately resulted in increased business.

An instinct, based on stories or past experiences, told the lower class Polish-Americans to beware of those who spoke good Polish or English ''because those educated slickers may easily outsmart you.''

Polish-American Jargon in Literature

Some of the foremost Polish writers, such as, Nobel prizewinners Henryk Sienkiewicz and Wladyslaw Reymont, incorporated expressions from the Polish-American jargon in their literary works. They did so not to ridicule the Polish people in America, but in order to portray their lives realistically.

The famous American author, journalist, and editor of the *American Mercury,* H. L. Mencken, did considerable research in American-English linguistics and as a result wrote about the Polish-American jargon in his book, entitled, *The American Language.*

However, a much broader, scholarly approach and recognition of the existence of a widely used Polish-American conversational language was made by Prof. Witold Doroszewski, who was head of the Polish Language Department at the University of Wisconsin in Madison before the outbreak of World War II. He published his studies and findings in a book entitled, *The Polish Language in USA,* printed by the Warsaw Educational Society in 1938. (The author who, after teaching in the United States, returned to Poland, was killed by the Nazis as were many other Polish scholars.)

In my sketches about the Polish blood in America's veins, written originally in Polish, I compiled twenty stories composed in the Polish-American jargon, covering almost every phase of Polish-American life. In addition, I assembled a dictionary comprising several thousand words and expressions.

I am omitting this in the English version. It would be necessary for the reader to be familiar with the Polish language to fully understand and appreciate this Polish-American jargon and its piquant, sometimes awkward or amusing characteristics.

V.

Early Polish Traces in America

The history of Polish participation in the discovery of America, Polish contributions to the growth of colonies, establishment of the United States and its development is preserved in legend and historical documents.

It is little known to the American public in general and even to the young generations of Americans of Polish descent because it is ignored in textbooks dealing with American history or if mentioned at all, then very briefly.

Findings of Polish-American Historians

Two prominent Polish-American historians searched old, forgotten documents, books, and encyclopedias to substantiate the history of Poles in America.

One of them was the late Father Waclaw Kruszka of Milwaukee. His historical findings were published by the Kuryer Polski Publishing Company in 1941.

The other was the late Mieczyslaw Haiman, former custodian of the Archives and Museum of the Polish Roman Catholic Union in Chicago, Ill., now existing there under the name of the Polish Museum. His works were written in Polish and English and were substantiated by thousands of authentic historical documents, found in public and private libraries and archives throughout the United States, Canada, and France.

In order to make the most interesting findings of these two Polish-American historians better known and easy to read, I am presenting excerpts from them herewith in the popular quiz method—the Socratic style of questions and answers.

When did the Poles first appear on the American continent?

According to the historical book *Antiquitates Americanae* two Polish knights settled in Greenland with Eric the Red in 985. That was 507 years before the discovery of America by Columbus.

How did the Poles join Eric the Red?

These two Polish warriors, named Tyrker and Wyzderwola, came to Denmark, bringing to the Danish king, Sweyn, the daughter of the Polish king, Mieczyslaw I, in marriage. At the Danish king's court, they got acquainted with Eric the Red and being of the same adventurous, warring nature, they became friends and joined his band in war expeditions. After Eric's assault on Iceland, they fled with him and settled in Greenland.

Which Pole allegedly took part in the discovery of America?

It was Tyrker, who became Leif Ericson's stepfather, after marrying the widow of Eric the Red. Leif Ericson's discovery of America, although still disputed, is gaining more and more historical acknowledgment.

What was Tyrker's share in Leif Ericson's triumph?

It is claimed that Leif discovered the American continent somewhere in the area of today's New England states. Tyrker, who accompanied him, discovered wild grapes growing there abundantly and taught the Norsemen how to make use of them.

Which Polish sailor was a rival of Columbus?

His Latin name was "Skolnus," from the Polish name "Jan z Kolna" (John from Kolno), where he was born in 1435. His parents wanted him to be a priest, but John ran away from his home in Poland and served on ships of various nations, hoping that someday he would get his own command.

Where did Skolnus meet Columbus?

He met Columbus at the famous school of navigators, established by the prince of Portugal, Henry the Navigator, in the Portuguese port of Sagras. He took part in voyages and expeditions directed by Henry the Navigator together with Columbus and many other sailors who became a part of the world's history. Among the navigation school pupils was another Polish sailor, Warnadowicz, who accepted the name of Fernandez.

How did the rivalry start?

After participating in many sea expeditions as pupils of Henry the Navigator and attaining the captain's rank, both Columbus and Skolnus presented a plan for an expedition across the Atlantic to Asia, to the king of Portugal, Alfonso V. When their plans were rejected, they separately approached other kings.

Which kings were interested in Skolnus' plan?

The Polish king, Casimir the Jagiellonian, and the Danish king, Christian I. The merchants of Cracow gave Skolnus strong support, but the Polish king was unable to finance the expedition since Poland at that time didn't have a fleet of its own. The Danish king, however, agreed to finance the expedition.

When did this expedition take place?

It left a Danish port in 1497. The fleet consisted of four sail ships. Skolnus was accompanied by his relative, Jacob Brzoza, who served in the court of the Danish king and was a go-between in the realization of the undertaking.

Did Skolnus reach America thinking it was Asia?

Documented history ends with his departure from Denmark. From various other sources and the stories of shipwrecked sailors, some historians claim that Skolnus' ships reached the shores of the present New England states, but on their way back to Denmark perished in a storm near Norway. Skolnus and several sailors managed to swim ashore, but he died from exhaustion before being able to write a report.

How many Polish sailors were with Columbus?

According to historian Thaddeus Moisey, the first sailor who volunteered to go with Columbus and, through his courageous example, helped Columbus to get other sailors to man his ships, was a Pole with the Spanish name of Francesco Fernandez. He was the son of the previously-mentioned Warnadowicz.

Historian Moisey adds: "Most probably there were other Polish sailors with Columbus who had accepted English, French, or Spanish names, according to the country in which they were living. Warnadowicz-Fernandez was killed in a fight with Indians on the island of Haiti."

When did the first wave of Polish immigrants come to America?

It is documented historically that the first group of Polish immigrants to settle in the newly founded English colony of Jamestown, Virginia, came in 1608, twelve years before the Pilgrims arrived in New England on the *Mayflower*.

What kind of people were these first Polish immigrants?

They were skilled workers, artisans and craftsmen, specialists in making pitch, tar, and by-products of pine trees; they knew how to make soap and glass; they knew how to make woodenware. Some of their names, recorded in old documents were: Nowicki, Stefanski, Mata, Sadowski, Zrenica, Machowski, Metus, Stojka, Kulawy, Malaszko, Micinski. In the old English documents, they were referred to as "Polonians."

Who brought these Polish immigrants to America?

England, through its colonization agency, the "Virginia Company of London." At first, England imported large amounts of pitch and timber, necessary for the building of ships, directly from Poland. Then it was decided that it would be more profitable to use American timber and bring the experienced Polish workers to the English colonies in America.

What were their most important contributions to America?

1. They contributed in establishing the first manufacturing and export center in America, in which they led as producers of the critically needed materials for shipbuilding as well as soap, glass, and woodenware.
2. They served as instructors for workers of English and other nationalities and were instrumental in establishing the first American apprentice system.
3. They showed great courage in fighting the Indians and two of them saved the life of Captain John Smith in a treason plot. Captain Smith was the first commander of the colony and gave full credit to the Polish accomplishments in his historical reports to the Virginia Company of London.

How were the Poles "rewarded?"

When the new governor gave the colony limited autonomy in 1618, the Poles were excluded from voting rights and other privileges on the pretext that they still owed the company for passage.

How did the Poles react?

They protested by proclaiming the first labor strike in America and demanding equality with other citizens.

Which documents and books describe the history of Poles in Jamestown?

The old English documents on the colonies, especially the following two: *The Voyages and Discoveries of Capt. John Smith in Virginia (1607-1609)* and *The Court Book of the Virginia Company of London.* Mention is made in the older editions of the *Encyclopedia Americana* (Vol. XIX), under the title, "History of Soap Making in America."

Did Polish immigration to America continue?

Yes, not only to Virginia, but from there to Pennsylvania, Kentucky, Ohio, and Indiana. It is hard to trace the first Polish settlers in historical documents, since their Polish names were usually changed by officials who wrote the documents in similarly sounding Anglo-Saxon spelling. The Poles accepted this because they didn't want to lose the properties acknowledged by the documents. Sometimes, however, a by-name was added, such as "Polonian," "Polander," or "Polacker."

What else can we assume from the old documents?

One document tells about Mathew Polander, killed on a farm during the Indian massacre of 347 whites living near Jamestown, in 1622. It shows that, at that time, Poles were not only artisans in Jamestown, but also farmers in the surrounding countryside.

In which other American colony did the Poles play an important part?

In the colony of New Holland, founded by the Dutch in 1626. An old Dutch document pictures as the main representatives of New Holland, three Hollanders, a Portuguese, a Swede, a Spaniard, a Frenchman, a Neapolitan, an Englishman, and a Pole, called Conrad Popolski.

What brought the Polish immigrants to New Holland?

Mostly religious intolerance and persecution of Polish Protestants or so-called dissidents. They were the gentry, scholars, and burghers who left the Roman Catholic church and joined the Protestant or other religious movements in the period of Reformation in Europe. The most prominent were the members of the sect known as "Polish Brothers," "Aryans," or "Polish Unitarians."

Who were the most prominent Poles in New Holland?

Besides the aforementioned Polish Brothers (Fratres Poloni), who have enriched the American world with scholarly works and who were the forerunners of the American Unitarian movement, the following should be mentioned:

Dr. Alexander Curtius (Latin name from Polish Kurcyusz), a famous scholar, who established the first American school on the high school level—an academy in New Amsterdam.

The Polish nobleman, Albert Zaborowski, who settled in New Amsterdam in 1662 and established the family which was later better known under the name of Zabriski and has been influential ever since, both in New York and New Jersey as bankers, lawyers, and writers.

Wojciech (Albert) Adamkiewicz, the most prominent building contractor in the times of Governor Stuyvesant.

Daniel Litchcoe (Liczko), owner of a tavern in which important personalities of that time resided temporarily. He was also a lieutenant in Governor Stuyvesant's army.

Which other colony included Poles?

The American colony of New Sweden, later taken by the Dutch and then by the English. Johnson's book: *The Swedes on the Delaware,* mentions the children of a Pole, Paul Malich. In 1651, a fort on the Delaware was given a Polish name; namely, "Fort Casimir" and part of the Dutch garrison was Polish. When the English took over, the Polish name was changed to "New Castle."

How many Poles were there among the religious sects seeking freedom in America?

It is hard to establish how many, but we know that some of the Poles became very prominent. In the document "History of the Evangelical Lutheran Church in the United States" (New York, 1907), mention is made that the first Lutheran pastor in New Amsterdam, after it was taken by the English, was a Pole from Glogow, Silesia, using the Latin name of Jacobus Fabritius (Fabrycjusz). There were also some Poles among the Quakers and the Mennonites in Pennsylvania.

Who were the most prominent Polish Moravians?

The Moravians, also known as Bohemian Brethren, found hospitality in Poland for over a century after being driven out of their native Bohemia. When the hospitality turned into persecution, they fled from Poland to Saxony and from there to America, colonizing in Pennsylvania. They founded the cities of Bethlehem, Nazareth, Lancaster, York, and others.

Among the Moravians were not only Czechs, but many polonized Germans and Poles. Some of the Poles were:

George Wenceslaus Golkowski, a Polish count, an accomplished surveyor and draftsman, who made many trips for the Moravians in Pennsylvania.

Sigismund Leskinsky (Leszczynski), warden of the Brethren's House at Bethlehem and founder of an ingenious brewery in that city. In one document it is mentioned that not only the beer was of superior quality, but the brewmaster came from a Polish royal family which previously gave the Moravians a haven in Poland.

Which Polish family is interwoven with the history of the American Midwest?

The Sadowski family, originating from the Polish nobleman, Anthony Sadowski, who came to America in 1714. He spoke seven languages and soon learned how to communicate with the Indians and gained their confidence.

His sons and grandsons followed in the footsteps of this Polish-American pioneer, although their Polish names were later changed to Sadowsky, Sandowski, Sandusky, etc. They established many trading posts in Ohio, Kentucky, and Indiana, which later became villages, towns, and cities, among others, Sandusky, Ohio.

Former United States President Theodore Roosevelt acknowledged the contributions of Sadowski in his book, *The Winning of the West*.

What was the role of Poles in the Revolutionary War of 1775-1783?

Hundreds of Poles from abroad and those who had settled or were born in America, participated in this war on the American side and a small group of Polish aristocrats fought on the English side.

Who were those on the English side?

The four most prominent ones were two members of the aristocratic family of Zabriski (Zaborowski), Count Grabowski, and an English army surveyor, Blaszkowicz. Blaszkowicz, however, has been referred to in a most flattering manner in American history, since his maps of America are a source of admiration and are regarded as important documents in the field of American history and geography.

Who were the Polish-Americans helping General Washington?

Among the Polish-American settlers, the most prominent

were those representing the old colonial families of Zabriski (with the exception of the two mentioned above), Sadowski, and Laski. The Zabriski house in Hackensack, New Jersey, was for sometime the headquarters of George Washington.

A Polish Jew, resident of Philadelphia, Pa., Chaim Salomon, gave General Washington his entire fortune, amounting to $650,000 to finance the revolution and also established credit for him with bankers in Spain, Holland, and France.

A prosperous Polish-American merchant in Charlestown, S. C., Samuel Harbowski, supplied the American revolutionary fleet with necessary merchandise.

Who were the Poles from abroad?

There were many of them and they played an important part in the American Continental Army because they had broad army and guerilla war experience. The most prominent among them were:

General Thaddeus Kosciuszko, an aide to General Washington, who directed the building of the fortifications at Saratoga and West Point. He was one of the founders of the famous "Society of the Cincinnati."

General Casimir Pulaski, who was appointed chief of cavalry and brigadier general for his distinguished service in the battle of Brandywine. Later he was commissioned by the Continental Congress to organize an independent corps of cavalry and light infantry, known as the Pulaski Legion.

Numerous Polish officers and soldiers, refugees from Poland, comprised the nucleus of the Pulaski Legion.

Other Polish officers and soldiers came with the Lauzun Legion, of the French army of General Rochambeau, which was credited as the decisive factor in the battle of Yorktown.

Felix Miklaszewicz, a Polish sea captain, commanded a group of Polish sailors, whose specialty was to destroy British ships. His schooner was registered in the documents under the name of "Prince Radziwill."

What happened to the Poles and Polish-Americans of the Revolutionary War?

Many of them died fighting for American independence, among them Gen. Pulaski. The Polish-Americans who survived the war, returned to their homes in America. Some of the Poles from abroad settled, after the war, in America (among them Miklaszewicz, who settled in Georgia). Others, like Gen. Kosciuszko, returned to Europe to join the revolutionary movements and wars for the independence of Poland.

What was the role of Poles in the war with England in 1812–1815?

It was a tragic and ironic fate of history that Polish soldiers fought on both sides.

On the American side were the Polish-American settlers.

On the English side were some Polish settlers in Canada, who were forced to join the English army, and there were the Polish prisoners-of-war from Napoleon's army which had been defeated by the English. They were given a choice of dying in English dungeons or joining the English army.

When did a large group of Polish insurgents land in the United States?

In 1834, Austria shipped to America, on a fleet of three ships, about 300 Polish insurgents against Russia, who had been imprisoned by Austria after crossing its border in retreat. They ranged in age from seventeen to sixty.

The United States Congress passed a bill to give these Polish refugees certain lands in Illinois to establish a Polish settlement. These plans were never realized. Unable to settle as a group, these Polish insurgents dispersed all over America.

How did they manage to make a livelihood?

Since most of them were well educated and spoke several languages, it wasn't hard for them to learn English. Soon some of them started to publish papers and books in English, dealing with Polish themes.

Some became teachers of foreign languages, music, painting, drawing, etc.

Some were given insignificant positions in various governmental bureaus in Washington.

Some joined the United States army and participated in the wars against the Indians.

Some former Polish cavalrymen or experienced horsemen became mail carriers in the Wild West.

In one known instance, a Polish priest-insurgent became a shoemaker in order to make a living.

Which of these Polish insurgents became better known in America?

A former Polish army officer and insurgent against Russia, Gustav Szulc, was one of the leaders in an American voluntary expedition to free Canada from English rule, and to annex it to the United States. He was taken prisoner by the English in the Battle under the Windmill in 1838 and was put to death by hanging.

A former major in the Polish insurgent army, Casper Tochman, became a prominent attorney-at-law, privileged to practice before the highest United States tribunal. He spoke to legislative bodies of various American states in defense of Poland and gave similar lectures in many cities. Later he settled in the South, joined the Confederacy and became a general of the "Polish Brigade" in the Civil War.

Henry Glowacki became a famous American lawyer. He is regarded as the founder of the city of Batavia, New York and was very active in American Democratic party politics.

Adam Gurowski, a Polish nobleman, became a political writer for the largest American newspapers and author of such books as: *Russia and It's People, America and Europe, Slavery in History.* Disgusted with the Vatican's attitude toward the Polish insurrection against Russia, he became a sharp critic of the Roman Catholic Church.

Joseph Karge, a refugee from the Polish insurrection of 1848, became famous as the organizer of the American educational system. In the *National Encyclopedia of American Biography,* he is cited as one of the best educators of that period. He was also a brigadier general in the Union forces in the Civil War.

Other Polish refugees from the tragic November insurrection of 1831 became known as foremost American educators, to wit:

Leopold Boeck, the founder of the first technological institute in America; Ludwik Bonczakiewicz, Artur Grabowski, Josef d'Alfons, and Dr. Kraitzer, a polonized Hungarian, who became dean of the Academy of Maryland and in 1837 published a book entitled: *The Poles in the United States.*

In the field of arts, the following Polish insurgents attained prominence: Julian Fontana and Adam Kurek as artist-musicians and Henry Dmochowski-Sanders as the sculptor who created the Pulaski monument in Washington, D.C.

There were others, like Joseph Truskolaski, an engineer and surveyor of lands in Louisiana and Utah; Captain Karol Radziminski, one of the American surveyors who marked the United States-Mexican border; Alex Raszewski and Alex Sengteller, renowned as excellent engravers; Ludwik Szpaczek and R. Thomain, distinguished physicians in New York, and Henryk Kalusowski, a prominent physician in Washington, D.C.

The young American culture was enriched by English translations from Polish literature done by Joseph Podbielski; A. A. Jakubowski, a Polish poet, mastered the English language in an incredibly short time and began to write English poetry. In 1842, Sobolewski, Wyszynski and Company began to publish a magazine in New York entitled, *Poland, Literary, Monumental and Picturesque,* and Martin Rosienkiewicz published the first English language manual for Polish people: *Dialogues to facilitate the acquisition of the English Language by Polish Emigrants.*

When was the first U.S. Congressmen of Polish extraction elected?

In 1849 in New York. His name was Lawrence (Wawrzyniec) Gebicki. He was born in Poland in 1793, a son of a blacksmith. With thousands of other Poles he joined the Polish legions of Napoleon. Taken prisoner of war by the English at Waterloo, instead of going to a dungeon or service in the English army, he managed, thanks to his trade, to get into a factory making knives and other steel products and got to be quite an expert.

He came to America in 1824 to work in a similar factory, becoming later a partner and then a sole owner.

VI

Formation of Parishes and Organizations

According to historian Mieczyslaw Haiman, up to the year 1850, Polish people in America were dispersed everywhere and there were few larger Polish settlements, except those mentioned in Chapter V.

The "Roll of Honor," an old document of the Civil War of 1861-65, records the existence of one of these smaller Polish communities. In it are listed the names of ten Polish soldiers and three officers from such a settlement in New Orleans, La.

This Polish settlement was founded by refugees, former volunteers in Napoleon's army. Disappointed by Napoleon, who ignored their dreams of marching into Poland, they deserted and came to America. This settlement was augmented later by other refugees.

Polish Liberals Predominated in Early Times

These Polish refugees and exiles were mostly intellectuals; they mingled freely with Americans of various national descent and were not interested in establishing Polish parishes or to be herded into separate ghettos.

First Polish Societies in the U.S.A.

The first Polish organizations in America were of secular and political character, embracing Poles regardless of religion, and including Poles of Jewish descent.

The name of the first Polish organization in the U.S.A. was, "Society of Poles in America," founded in New York in 1842. Among its aims was dissemination of information among Americans about the revolutionary movements for the liberation of Poland and giving financial support to these movements.

About ten years later, another Polish-American organization was created in New York under the name of "Democratic Society of Polish Exiles in America." It was a component of an American political organization entitled, "Universal Democratic Republicanism," which was a forerunner of the Republican party.

The aims of the Polish component were partly the same as in the other organization, but in addition its purpose was to encourage Polish immigrants to participate in American political life.

Although most of the Polish refugees were religious and Roman Catholics, they were not anxious to organize Roman Catholic parishes because they were angry at the Vatican for condemning the Polish insurrection against the Russian Tsar, on the grounds that all authority derives from God, including the authority of the Russian Tsar.

Some Polish Roman Catholic priests, who took part in the 1830-31 insurrection and after its failure fled to America, met with a hostile attitude from the American Roman Catholic hierarchy. Under such conditions, instead of organizing their fellow exiles into parishes, they turned to other occupations.

The Polish Gold Rush to America

One of the liberal Poles, whose name is written in golden letters in the history of early America, was Dr. Felix

Wierzbicki. As a young refugee, he was taken under the guardianship of an American family. Thanks to their help, he was able to attend an American university and later became a prolific English writer and a doctor of medicine. He was one of the founders of the first medical society in California and author of *Essay on History of Medicine*.

In his articles, published in American newspapers in the East, he criticized the hostile attitude of the Vatican toward the Polish insurrection against the Tsar, and the role played by Polish Jesuits in Poland.

This resulted in his persecution. Disgusted, he left for San Francisco, California, and settled there in 1847. At that time there was in San Francisco, a small colony of former Polish insurgents, who after arriving in America, joined the U.S. Army and participated in the war with Mexico in 1845.

In 1849, Dr. Wierzbicki wrote his first English book, describing California under the long but interesting title: *"California As It Is and As It May Be, or A Guide of The Gold Region"* (George D. Lyman—*Wierzbicki, The Book and the Doctor*, The Grabhorn Press, San Francisco, 1933).

His book about California and its gold, reached Poland in a Polish translation. It caused many Polish people to risk the dangerous travel to America in quest of California gold. They are known in history as the Polish argonauts. Most of them did not reach California. Without adequate means to travel across the American continent and Indian territories, they gave up and settled in Texas, Michigan, and Wisconsin.

Another Emigration Wave From Poland to America

In contrast to the previous arrivals, this new wave consisted of Polish peasants, hungry for land and looking for better opportunities in life. A Polish Roman Catholic priest, Rev. Leopold Moczygemba, who was sent by the Franciscan Order, together with four German Franciscans, to Texas in 1851, was instrumental in bringing them there.

This large group of Polish people arrived successfully in Texas in 1854, where Rev. Moczygemba bought for them a large tract of land. This land was divided and resold to the new arrivals. Soon the land was put under cultivation and cleared of the snakes infesting the region. A church was built and the parish was named "Panna Marya" (Virgin Mary) to commemorate the famous Church of St. Mary in Cracow, Poland. This settlement exists to this day.

This first group of Polish peasant immigrants who came with the intention of settling on farms was followed by other groups and other Polish Roman Catholic priests, who organized new parishes and built churches or at least small chapels in many localities in Texas.

According to historian Father W. Kruszka, a Polish Roman Catholic parish existed already in 1852 in Paris, Michigan. The name of this settlement was changed later to Pardeville.

Polish Participation in the Civil War (1861-1865)

Most of the Polish soldiers in that war came from the state and city of New York. Two former Polish insurgents, Julian Allen and W. Krzyzanowski, organized a regiment called the "Polish Legion." (Julian Allen was of Jewish descent, therefore, he was, like many other similar Poles in America, a victim of prejudice in some Polish-American circles). Krzyzanowski was made a colonel and later a brigadier general.

Another New York Pole, J. Smolinski, assisted by his eighteen-year old son, organized a regiment of cavalry, similar to the famous Polish uhlans, called "United States Lancers." Due to internal discord, this regiment was later dissolved and its separate detachments were attached to various New York regiments.

The Polish-American historian, M. Haiman, found about 1,700 Polish-sounding names of soldiers and officers in the

Union army. It is difficult to guess how many other Poles or Americans of Polish descent, whose names were Americanized, changed, or didn't sound Polish, were in the Union armed forces.

However, it is known that three Poles were made generals in the Union army, namely:

The aforementioned, Gen. W. Krzyzanowski, organizer and commander of the "Polish Legion."

General Joseph Karge, whose other accomplishments as an educator were described in Chapter V.

The least known as being a Pole, because of a German-sounding name, was Gen. Alfred Schoepf, who was born in Cracow, Poland in 1822. He was an officer in the Austrian army, joined the Hungarian revolution of liberals against the Austrian regime, then fled to Turkey, where he was given a high military post. From Turkey he came to America, joined the Union Army and distinguished himself in the battle of Perryville. After the war he was a member of the highest military tribunal in Washington.

Polish Soldiers in the Confederate Army

Many Poles who settled in the South served in the Confederate army. There was a "Polish Brigade" organized by Gen. Tochman, a former Polish officer in the Polish insurrection of 1830-31, whose previous activity as a speaker and attorney-at-law in Washington is described in Chapter V.

The commander of the "Polish Brigade" was another former Polish insurgent, Col. Vincent Sulakowski, an engineer by profession. Later Gen. Magruder gave him the command over the seventh brigade, consisting of the Second Lousiana Infantry Regiment.

Plans to Form a Polish Army for the South

Toward the end of the Civil War, President Lincoln,

afraid of provoking the powerful Tsar of Russia, handed over to the Russians two leaders of the Polish insurrection, who had fled to America.

Col. Sulakowski decided to take advantage of the indignation caused among Poles and introduced to the leaders of the South a plan to enlist about 30,000 former insurgents, experienced officers and soldiers, exiles in Europe, in a Polish army to support the South. His plan was approved. He was given money for necessary expenses and to buy ships. He was unable, however, to penetrate the blockade, his ship was caught by the naval forces of the North and his dreams of bringing a Polish army to the rescue of the South were frustrated.

Polish Women-Samaritans in the Civil War

Among the nurses with the army of the North were two sisters, Polish nuns from the Order of Sisters of Mercy. They were of the Klimkiewicz family, relatives of Gen. Kosciuszko. One of the nuns, Sister Veronica, while taking care of a wounded Confederate soldier recognized him as her own brother.

This was only one of the numerous tragic episodes, showing Polish people taking part in wars opposite one another.

Another Polish woman, Mrs. Sosnowski, widow of a Polish exile in America together with her daughters conducted a private school for girls in Columbia, S.C. During the Civil War, her school was changed into a workshop for making bandages and other Samaritan supplies. Mrs. Sosnowski herself served as a nurse with the Confederate Army.

Polish Parishes and Churches Spring Up After the Civil War

The "Great Polish Exodus" to America began after the Civil War and lasted until the outbreak of World War I. The great majority of these immigrants were plain country folk, peasants and laborers, suffering from all kinds of oppression, mainly poverty. Most of these immigrants were unable to shift for themselves. They needed leadership and guidance. They wanted to stay together with people of their own religion, clan or region, so they started to organize parishes.

To establish and administer these parishes, various Polish Roman Catholic orders began to compete in sending their priest-organizers to America.

The Growth of Polish Secular Societies

While on the one hand, the Polish immigrants were being organized into parishes and church societies, on the other hand, the intellectuals began to organize more and more secular socieities. Friction arose between these two camps.

The activities and aims of the parish and the secular organizations were different. The Polish people in the parishes were interested in religious devotions, the welfare of their parish and church, and were trying to make a better life for themselves than they had had in the old country. Their interest in the insurrections and liberation movements in Poland was secondary if not entirely nil. Many of them looked upon the Polish gentry as oppressors of the Polish peasants just as much as if they were Russians, Germans, or Austrians.

The members of Polish secular societies, however, were interested in giving help to the insurgents and rebels against the three powers ruling Poland.

The Founding of the "Polish Roman-Catholic Union"

Among the Polish Roman Catholic priests who came to America after 1863 were some fervent Polish patriots. They knew that in order to be acknowledged by the Roman Catholic hierarchy in America, consisting mostly of Irish and German bishops, they must have a strong Polish organization behind them.

So in the year 1872, they organized, in Chicago, the Polish Roman-Catholic Union. The aims of this first Polish-American organization on a national scale were as follows:

"To guard the Polish immigrant against the loss of Roman Catholic faith and Polish nationality and to erect and improve Polish Roman Catholic parochial schools in America."

Polish Liberals Form the Polish National Alliance

In 1880, the independent Polish liberal societies decided to unite into one large organization. In answer to an appeal sent from Switzerland by the leader of the Polish liberation movement, Agaton Giller, they banded together under the name of the "Polish National Alliance" which today is the largest Polish-American fraternal organization in America.

Its aims at the beginning were as follows:

1. To help the Polish cause of liberation.
2. To raise the Polish immigrants to a higher level by promoting learning and knowledge.
3. To serve as a dignified Polish representation in the U.S.A.
4. To acquaint the Americans with accurate information about Poland, Polish history, literature, and culture.
5. To serve as a bridge between Poland and America.
6. To bring up future Polish-American generations so that they would not be ashamed of their national origin.

Polish Women's Alliance

The third largest Polish-American fraternal organization, the Polish Women's Alliance was founded in 1898 by progressive women interested in greater freedom and a more important role for females in Polish communities.

These three largest Polish-American organizations had and still have their headquarters in Chicago. All three had or still have leaders of high ideals and some shrewd operators. A strong rivalry existed between them in the past—but now it has subsided and, at least on the surface, the high-level officials are interested in co-operation, primarily on matters of mutual financial interest.

Polish Organizational Fever

The multifarious character of Polish people, and more precisely the ambitions of egotistic leaders, is illustrated plainly by the multitude of Polish-American organizations which began to spring up, starting in the second part of the nineteenth century; each one of them professing similar aims but competing or feuding with each other.

The masses of Polish immigrants were eager to join an organization where they could have freedom to express themselves or just listen to others' expressions, since they had had no such opportunity in the old country.

"Polish Armed Forces in America"

Don't let this title shock you. There was such an organization, formed at the end of the nineteenth century, but it was a comic opera parochial army, used mainly for decorative purposes in church processions and other parochial affairs.

The various, separate components of this army had such titles as "St. Stanislaus Cavalry" or "St. Joseph's Artillery," etc. The members of these so-called military units were dressed in brilliant uniforms often resembling former Polish or Napoleonic soldiers. All had sabers and all had ranks of officers. There was not a private or even a sergeant in the whole army. They gave splendor to church processions or parades around the parish and provided an interesting attraction to the curious onlookers. Usually their roll calls, rituals, drills, and maneuvers were held or ended at a nearby Polish saloon and had nothing in common with military operations.

Polish-American Youth Organizations

In contrast to this comic opera army, there were organizations, embracing many youthful Polish-Americans and older instructors and advisors, with the aim of providing volunteers for Poland's war of liberation, if such an occasion arose.

The first one on a larger scale was the "Alliance of Polish Youth in America" organized in 1890. Very active and helpful to Poland before and during World War I, it later disintegrated, since "youth" is only temporary and since it was based on ideals and not on a fraternal system of life insurance.

Polish Falcons of America

This used to be a dynamic Polish-American youth and adult organization, composed of Falcon nests in all larger Polish communities. The first nest was organized in Chicago in 1886. The outward aim was gymnastics, similar to the Swiss or German "Turners." The real aim was to keep the body and mind in good health for the purpose of organizing potential fighters for the liberation of Poland.

This objective was fulfilled to a certain extent during World War I. Some of the members of the Polish Falcons in America, divided at that time into two camps joined the Polish Legions of Gen. Pilsudski, fighting on the side of Austria against Russia. Others formed the nucleus of the 20,000 volunteers from America who joined the Polish Army in France, fighting on the side of the Allies against Germany.

Thanks to the introduction of the fraternal life insurance system, the Polish Falcons are still in existence today, but the program of gymnastics is kept up in relatively few nests. In many cases the activity of the Falcon nests is centered upon bowling or other sports, or social activities and drinking at the bar. This applies to many other Polish-American clubs and societies.

Polish-American Political Organizations

Since 1852, when the first Polish component of the "Universal Democratic Republicanism" was organized in New York, Polish-American political clubs or Polish-American citizens clubs were and are functioning in various cities with a larger Polish population.

The only prominent, strictly Polish political organization in America was the "Alliance of Polish Socialists." For some time it had ties with the American Socialist Party, but the friendly relations were broken off when the American Socialists refused to support the liberation movement in partitioned Poland.

The activities of the "Alliance of Polish Socialists in America" had very little to do with the radical programs of some American Socialists. To be sure, it gave its support to the American labor union movement, the fight for an eight-hour day, the miners', steel, and garment workers' strikes, since many Polish workers were involved, but its chief purpose of existence was twofold:

First, and above all, to give financial help to the militant Socialist Party in Poland in its fight for the liberation of the country.

Secondly, to raise the Polish people in the U.S.A. to a higher level by encouraging them to read, learn, and think for themselves. A Polish Peoples University was organized, giving a series of popular lectures on Sundays. In these activities a very sharp friction arose between them and the Polish Roman Catholic clergymen. After World War I, internal frictions broke out among the Polish-American Socialists and the organization disintegrated.

Other Organizations

Thousands of singing, dancing, dramatic, literary, professional, and social clubs were born and died.

There are now more and more Polish-American organizations whose business is conducted mostly or entirely in the English language: Polish-American clubs of federal, state, and city employees; of senior citizens; of a social and a cultural variety; of Polish-American professional men and of some components of Polish fraternal organizations, especially the Polish National Alliance, who distinguish themselves from the Polish-speaking groups by using the English language. Examples of these are the Chicago Society, Milwaukee Society, etc.

Polish-American war veterans are mainly members of various American veterans associations. However, some are in three separate Polish organizations, active more or less on a national scale, namely: the Polish Legion of American Army Veterans, the Association of Polish Army Veterans in America, and the organization of Polish Combatants.

VII

The Evolution of Polish Immigrants

The Polish settlements, built up around churches and parishes, gave birth to the first Polish-American merchants and politicians, excepting, of course, the early immigrants who were active in American commerce, trade, other business activities, and politics before Polish parishes were organized.

The Polish Saloon Has Its History

The prototype of the Polish-American merchant and politician was the saloon keeper. This type of business did not need special schooling and, if the man had the right qualities, he didn't need much of an investment. The breweries and liquor firms were ready to finance him.

In Polish-American history, a saloon was a sort of national institution. It was regarded by many immigrants as a sort of temple in which to celebrate certain occasions. The saloon keeper was a man to be entrusted with the most intimate secrets, gripes, griefs, sorrows, lamentations, and complaints. He was the man to give advice, credit, and sometimes even financial loans. On occasion, he would bail those who had been arrested for drunkenness or causing a domestic brawl, out of jail.

Soon the saloon keeper became a rival of the priest as an advice giver and even more important in the field of politics, telling the Polish people how they should vote.

At the beginning, the saloon keeper was just a flunky for a middleman, the connecting link with influential politicians, mostly Irish. Then, some of them took over the go-between job while others became influential politicians themselves, having direct connections with those in power.

To keep a more or less harmonious relation with the priest of the parish, the saloon keeper played the role of a church benefactor, paying for his saloon-keeping sins with donations, prizes for church bazaars, or other similar gifts.

Now the old Polish saloon keeper has been transformed into a modern tavern keeper. Many things have changed in the conduct of his business. He doesn't have the former political power anymore, yet in precinct and ward politics he's still very often an influential person. Candidates for various offices, even judges, looking for support of Polish-American voters see to it that their signs are displayed in the taverns and most of them consider it a duty to visit the tavern keeper before election time and buy drinks for all present at the bar.

The Beginning of Polish-American Commerce

After the saloon keepers, little grocery shops, meat markets, variety, and clothing stores began to spring up in the area of the newly founded parishes. The new ventures were started by the more versatile and courageous or shrewd parishioners, who had accumulated some money and had the desire to go into business instead of working in the factory.

Some of them had certain business abilities or experiences, others could hardly read, write, or count; yet, they had very helpful instructors, namely salesmen, mostly Jewish, who showed them how to make a display window and taught them the fundamentals of business.

Then came the Polish craftsmen, carpenters, cabinetmakers, metal workers, etc., who had learned their trade in Poland or completed their training upon arriving in America. Slowly they began to venture into businesses of their own; sometimes on a part-time basis, sometimes full-time, establishing their repair shops or workshops near the parish, where they were known and trusted. Sometimes the whole family took part in the enterprise.

To propagandize the strictly Polish or Catholic character of their businesses and to draw Polish people away from Jewish stores, such slogans were used as: "Countryman to countryman!"; "Buy only in a Christian store!" Polish-American chambers of commerce and trade associations were formed under similar slogans in cities such as Chicago, Detroit, Buffalo, and others.

The era of the greatest development of such stores, based to a large extent on nationalistic, religious, and anti-Semitic slogans, was in the years of 1915 to 1930. According to a Polish directory published in Chicago in 1928, the number of Polish business firms in that area alone was as follows:

Various small stores—about 3,000; small grocery stores—1,500; large grocery stores—1,000; butcher shops—1,000; barber and beauty shops—1,000; tailor shops—1,000; real estate offices—1,000; hardware shops—600; bakeries—500; drug stores—250; funeral parlors—250; and many lesser ones. The number of saloons was not given.

From the round numbers, we may assume that they were mostly estimates instead of being taken from a precise survey. Even so, these statistics give a vivid picture of the former Polish ghetto in Chicago. Most notable is the fact that among thousands of various, strictly Polish stores and shops, there were only three Polish bookstores. However, books were circulated in large quantities by some Polish newspapers, offering them as subscription premiums.

Changes Have Taken Place

The old slogans used to propagandize Polish commerce

and trade in America failed completely. The Polish-Americans educated in American schools and active in trade and commerce prefer to use the accepted American methods of selling.

There are still some stores and shops owned by Polish-Americans which depend exclusively on strictly Polish support. Most of the larger ones do business regardless of nationality, race, or religion and employ salespeople who can speak Polish and English. The largest number of Polish-Americans engaged in trade and commerce are now partners, managers, or salesmen and saleswomen in large, all-American concerns, chain stores, etc. Those who speak Polish or understand the ways of Polish people are always in demand by firms if their outlets are located in Polish neighborhoods.

The First Polish-American Industrialists and Professionals

With the exception of those few, who upon arrival in this country already had experience or preparatory education in industry or various professions, most of the Polish immigrants had to climb the ladder to higher positions the hard way.

First, there were those who by their nature were ambitious, industrious, intelligent, and ingenious, but lacked formal training or education. They took full advantage of opportunities offered them in America. Having strong will power, they spent their time, after working in a factory, on self-education, correspondence courses, lectures, or attending evening schools. They saved every penny they could, instead of spending it foolishly, as did many others in saloons, for a good time and recreation. Out of such stock came the first Polish-American organizers of building and loan associations, some of whom later became bankers, founders of small shops (some of which are now large factories), and so on and on.

Secondly, there were the younger ones, who came here with their parents or on their own. They were without financial means to permit pursuing higher education. So, at first, they worked hard, mostly as plain laborers in factories and, after saving enough money, they began their studies, working their way through universities as busboys, waiters, or taking whatever work opportunity presented itself in order to pay for their school expenses. Out of such stock came the first Polish-American professors, doctors, lawyers, and other professionals.

As an example of "guts" and accomplishments of some Polish immigrants, here's a short life story of a young Polish immigrant who eventually became a professor at Harvard University and later president of the board of trustees of the Polish-American cultural institution, "Kosciuszko Foundation."

His name was Stephen Mizwa (originally Mierzwa). He came to this country at the age of eighteen in 1910. At the beginning, he worked in a basket factory during the day and at night attended classes at the Carnegie Institute in Northampton, Mass. Later, while working part-time, he attended the American International College in Springfield, Mass. He received his B.A. from Amherst and his M.A. from Harvard University where he became a professor in 1923.

Most Immigrants Preferred to Send Their Children to a Factory than to School

Unlike the exemplary immigrants of Jewish faith, who did their utmost to give their children a higher education, most of the Polish immigrants preferred to send them to a factory, even when they were of school age.

These conditions have changed now for the better and more and more young Polish-Americans are being graduated from colleges and universities, attaining prominent places in professional, scientific, and business fields. The thinking of the peasant immigrants was based on a narrow-minded desire to obtain prosperity as fast as possible for the parents. They were concerned only about the present and not thinking of the future.

In those times, the parents received the pay envelopes of

their sons and daughters, who were working in a factory or shop. The youngsters received a small amount for spending money. If the family was large and, usually a Polish-American family was large, the parents invested the family's paychecks in building and loan associations or acquired property for income purposes. However, when a daughter or son got married, they gave them a certain share of the accumulated money for a wedding present or dowry. Now these conditions no longer exist.

The Effect of Two Wars and Prohibition

It may be said that the two World Wars created a number of big Polish-American industrialists and Prohibition, a number of prosperous Polish-American businessmen.

The small shops, previously established by Polish immigrants, who were craftsmen and artisans, grew into large shops thanks to the subcontracts received from large American firms, overloaded with war orders. Gradually, the sons of Polish immigrants, born and educated in America, who had learned the fundamentals of the trade, working in their fathers' shops, took over the management. Many of them succeeded in modernizing and enlarging the plants, but the Polish-American character usually was retained by employing mostly Polish-American workers.

As to prohibition being a factor in the growing number of Polish-American businesses, the story is as follows: In the era of Prohibition, many Polish people tried their luck in the dangerous and illegal business of making and selling "moonshine." Some were caught by federal agents, some were "eliminated" by gangsters, controlling at that time this illicit industry, but some survived and made a lot of money. This money was invested later in lawful business ventures. The management of these ventures was usually taken over by the younger and better-educated or professionally-trained members of the family. And again, the Polish-American character of these firms was usually retained; sometimes by keeping the Polish name of the firm; sometimes by major employment of Polish-American workers, or by dealing mostly with Polish-American customers.

The Evolution of Polish-American Politicians

As stated before, the first Polish-American politician or politician's flunky was the saloon keeper. Naturally the parish priest had and has his own place in politics, but it is on a higher level. He is more like an invisible man, pulling the strings.

Gradually, more and more Polish-Americans began to take part in politics, taking advantage of the large sections of Polish-American voters. They can be divided into two main categories: those who represent primarily the interest of the Roman Catholic church and those who are more or less independent of the Roman Catholic clergy. They value their support, but don't ask for their sanction in running for political offices. And this trend in Polish-American politics is growing steadily.

VIII

The Polish-American Press and Journalists

I had my first glimpses of the Polish-American press while still a young boy living in the "old country," the part of Poland called Silesia (at that time under the Austrian occupation and now partly in Poland and partly in Czechoslovakia).

My father was the publisher and editor of a Polish newspaper, *Voice of the Silesian People*. Most of my after-school hours were spent in the newspaper office and print shop, helping out with wrapping, addressing, trips to the post office, etc.

My father's newspaper was sent out to Polish newspapers published abroad and, in exchange, we received Polish newspapers published in various parts of the world including the U.S.A. and Canada.

At that time, America was synonymous to me with Indians and exciting Buffalo Bill stories. The giant format of the Polish-American newspapers in contrast to our local Polish tabloid publications was impressive. But the unfamiliar expressions and stories, pertaining to life and frictions existing among the Poles living in America, made it hard for me to understand what it was all about. Little did I dream at that time that in a not too distant future, I myself would become a part of this strange Polish-American press and Polish-American life.

My Experiences in the Polish-American Newspaper Field

I came to the U.S.A. with my parents in 1911 and in 1914, at the age of seventeen, I began to contribute stories to Polish-American newspapers. In addition, I got interested in the Polish-American amateur and professional theater.

At the age of nineteen, I got my first full-time job as an all-around apprentice, reporter, and proofreader with a Polish daily and weekly, the *Ameryka-Echo,* published in Toledo, Ohio, where my father was a coeditor.

During World War I, at the age of twenty, I joined the Polish army in France, which was being organized in the U.S.A. as an allied component of the French army in the war against Germany. I was sent to a training camp in Canada, then to France, and finally to Poland, where I took part in the Polish-Russian war in the Ukraine. After being brought back to America on the U.S. transport ship, "Pocahontas," I returned to my Polish-American journalistic work, acquiring also, for security reasons, the sideline trade of a printer.

I worked as a Polish-American newsman, coeditor, editor, publisher, or printer in the Polish communities of Chicago, Milwaukee, Toledo, Cleveland, New York, Scranton, Wilkes-Barre, and many others. My specialty was the observation and review of the Polish-American press and Polish-American life.

The Polish-American Press Before and Now

The years just before, during, and after World War I, were the golden years for the Polish-American press. Not counting the numerous weeklies and other periodicals, twenty-four dailies were printed here in the Polish language, among them six in Chicago, three in Detroit, New York, and Milwaukee, two in Cleveland and Buffalo, others in Boston, Jersey City, Pittsburgh, Wilkes-Barre, and Toledo. Now, in 1977, only three dailies remain. These are printed partially in Polish and partially in English and published in the cities of Chicago, Detroit, and in the New York area.

A Brief History of the Polish-American Press

The following details about the first Polish publications in America are based on the memoirs of a pioneer Polish-American journalist, Henry Nagiel, published in 1894 and the writings of Stanislaus Osada.

It was in 1863 when the first Polish newspaper and print shop was established in the U.S.A. Since a Polish paper cannot be printed with regular English type because it needs letters with various accents, dots, and hooks, it was necessary to have a print shop that possessed these materials and equipment.

The name of the founder of the first Polish newspaper and printshop in the U.S.A. was Schriftgieser. He was a Polish immigrant of Jewish descent. The name of this newspaper was *Echo from Poland*. It appeared from 1863 to 1865, and was printed in New York.

The second Polish-American newspaper with a Polish print shop appeared in 1870 and was called *Orzel Polski* (The Polish Eagle). The founder and editor was a former Roman Catholic priest by the name of Szczepankiewicz who had disassociated himself from the church and got married, thereby bringing upon himself the wrath of the church.

It is to be noted that the first two Polish-American newspapers were strictly independent, liberal, and devoted entirely to Polish matters and causes.

The First Polish-American Journalistic War

The third paper, *Pielgrzym* (The Pilgrim), started its publication in 1872 and was published in the print shop of the defunct *Polish Eagle* but in 1874, after moving to Chicago, it changed its name to *Gazeta Katolicka* (The Catholic Gazette).

At that time there was already a Polish paper with a print shop in Chicago called *Gazeta Polska* (The Polish Gazette), founded in 1873.

The year 1874 marks the beginning of a dogged war of rivalry between the Chicago Polish-American newspapers which lasted for a long time. At that time the *Polish Gazette* was the defender of the newly formed Polish-American organizations, independent of the clergyman's rule and the *Catholic Gazette* was against all "rebels" trying to organize independent societies outside the parish without the protectorate of the clergy.

The "Radical" and the "Christian" Press

With the establishment of more and more Polish-American print shops, Polish publications began to multiply rapidly.

In those times it took only a small amount of cash and some credit at the printers to start a newspaper.

The publishers were divided into two general camps. If a clergyman, his relative, or supporter published a paper, it was called a Christian paper. On the other hand, if the publisher was more independent, if he dared to criticize conditions in a parish or support such movements as establishment of an eight-hour workday, abolishment of exploitation of children and women, organization of unions, etc., he was accused of publishing a radical paper.

Some Samples of Polish-American "Radical" Press

In 1876 a plain, Polish self-educated worker invested his savings in establishing a newspaper, *Przyjaciel Ludu* (The Peoples Friend), which was called liberal and progressive. It didn't last long. In the same year, two Polish shoemakers and one tailor pooled their savings together to publish a newspaper in New York under the name of *Kuryer Nowoyorski* (The New

York Courier). They hired editors from the unemployed Polish intelligentsia who, at that time, could be had a dime a dozen. This publication lasted two years and was followed by another, *Ogniwo* (The Link), and then still another, *Zgoda,* (Harmony), which later moved to Chicago and was transformed into the official organ of the Polish National Alliance.

But there was a really "red" Polish publication in New York in 1887 because it was printed on red-colored paper. It's name was *Ognisko* (The Hearth). The office of this paper was known as the headquarters for the Polish "Bohemia" and intelligentsia; their meetings were held there, card playing, and drinking took place there, and many Polish "Bohemians" spent their nights there, sleeping on U.S. Mail sacks. This publication also lasted about two years, but many of those "Bohemians" later served as editors of other Polish newspapers, including the so-called Christian publications.

The Polish-American Daily Newspapers

From 1863 to 1888, Polish-American publications were as a rule financial failures and didn't last very long. Most of the dailies, established afterwards were more fortunate.

The first Polish-American daily which turned out to be a financial success for many years to come was the Milwaukee *Kuryer Polski* (The Polish Courier) established in 1888 by Michael Kruszka, a graduate of an American business college, an insurance agent by profession and for some time a Wisconsin assemblyman and senator. He was so successful and esteemed as a publisher that in 1909, he was elected president of the Milwaukee Daily Newspaper Publishers Association, notwithstanding the fact that his newspaper was published in the Polish language and was condemned violently by the Roman Catholic hierarchy.

It was considered a "radical" paper by a number of Roman Catholic bishops because it didn't discriminate against those Poles who were not Roman Catholic, and because it fought discrimination against Polish nationality in the Roman Catholic church in America.

In about 1912, *Kuryer Polski,* together with twelve other Polish-American newspapers, was blacklisted by certain pillars of the Polish Roman Catholic clergy and immediately thereafter, Archbishop Messmer of Milwaukee and the bishops of Green Bay, Superior, LaCrosse, Marquette, Michigan, St. Cloud, Minn., Grand Rapids, Mich., and Toledo, Ohio, issued pastoral letters forbidding the faithful to read the "radical" Polish newspapers under the pain of forfeiting their rights to all church services, including absolution, the sacrament of marriage, the last rites for the dying, and Catholic burial.

This started a lot of bitterness and warring among Polish-Americans and instead of destroying the independent Polish newspapers, made them more popular and stronger.

The keenest rivalry and war took place among the Polish dailies in Chicago, considering themselves as leaders of the Polish-American press.

A Polish Publisher Who Made A Million

Most Polish dailies had to be subsidized by rich individuals, organizations, or donations of readers.

There were, however, some clever Polish-American publishers who made smaller or larger fortunes. The most prosperous one was A. A. Paryski, the publisher of the *Ameryka-Echo,* a weekly and later, in addition, a daily, established in 1889 in Toledo, Ohio.

This publisher, who started his business with a very small capital investment was later regarded as a Polish millionaire. What made his financial success possible where many others have failed? First of all, he was an experienced American printer, while most other Polish-American publishers knew very little or nothing about the printing business.

He also understood the needs of the Polish immigrants.

They were hungry for the Polish printed word, for honest advice, for an opportunity for self-expression, which was provided them in a large section of the paper, under the headline, "Voice of Readers." They liked not only extensive news from the homeland about events occurring in the towns and villages from which they came, but also the helpful information about pitfalls, set for the credulous Polish immigrant by dishonest leaders, schemers, and politicians—especially those blowing the Polish patriotic trumpets.

He was a first class organizer. There were, at that time, hundreds of more or less educated Polish people, describing themselves as "intelligentsia", looking for suitable employment. He hired them as "educational agents," sending them all over America to sell subscriptions to his newspaper and popular Polish books which his rotary presses printed by the hundreds of thousands.

In addition, he invested the money he made on his Polish newspaper and books in other successful American business ventures.

Another Successful Publication in Stevens Point, Wisconsin

Among those who made the publishing of a Polish newspaper a financial success for quite a long time were the Worzalla brothers of Stevens Point, Wis., publishers of the *Gwiazda Polarna* (Polaris or North Pole Star).

In 1891, one of the brothers, Stephen Worzalla, upon learning the printing trade in America, established a paper under the name of *Rolnik* (Farmer) for the numerous Polish farmers living at that time around Stevens Point. Several years later, together with his brother, Joseph, they bought a print shop in Stevens Point and started to publish the *"Polaris."* Next to the *Ameryka-Echo* it was the largest Polish weekly in America and it still exists, in 1977.

600-800 Polish Newspapers in the U.S.A.

The total number of Polish-language newspapers published at various times in America is estimated to be at from 600 to 800. Not many remain in existence in 1977. Most of those still in existence are organizational publications, often with predominantly English text. Some publications devoted to Polish-American matters are now printed entirely in English.

Observations on Polish-American Journalists

The first Polish-American journalists were, in the majority, idealists, devoted to one thought: to lift the Polish immigrant to a higher level of life, education, and enlightment. They were underpaid and exploited by many publishers. Frustrated and disillusioned, some of them became alcoholics and died tragically.

Some had higher, some lesser formal education, but mostly they were self-educated men, active not only as newspaper writers and reporters, but as lecturers, advisers, organizers, or prominent members of clubs, societies, literary, and theatrical groups. They had close contacts with all kinds of Polish people; those working in factories, mines, foundries and steel mills, garment industry, and on farms. They ate with them and drank with them, attended their meetings, parties, and weddings. And, sometimes, they walked with them, during strikes, on picket lines.

A new breed of American-born descendents of Polish immigrants, graduates of American schools of journalism, is now employed by the English-language American press. Newspapers published in cities with a large Polish-American population employ those having knowledge of the Polish language and Polish-American affairs, for assignments pertaining to news and stories describing life in Polish-American neighborhoods.

As yet, there aren't too many outstanding Polish-American editors of the English-language American press. As I remember, the most prominent one, during my time, was Anthony Czarniecki, editor of the *Chicago Daily News* and member of the Chicago Board of Education in the 1920's.

IX

Polish-Americans in the Theater, Films, on Radio and T.V.

In the first three decades of the twentieth century, the Polish theater in America had its years of great artistic achievements, and it enjoyed even greater popularity when it was less artistic, but stressed entertainment in the form of vaudeville, comedy, and burlesque.

Only nostalgic memories now remain! The Polish-American theatrical field could be divided into three main categories: The amateur, the semiprofessional, and the professional theater.

The Amateur Theater

The amateur theatrical productions, presented in parish and private halls, were staged on different levels. Some were very primitive, some elaborate.

Very often the plays were based on religious events and lives of Catholic saints. The Nativity plays were the most spectacular, especially when given a Polish national character, with a title such as "Polish Bethlehem" or "Polish Nativity Play." In such plays, King Herod was presented as the Russian Tsar, or German Kaiser, or Prussian Prince Bismarck, typifying the oppressors of Poland. The three kings were portrayed by images of well-known personalities, friendly to the Polish people, and the visitors and shepherds paying homage at the manger were represented by historical Polish figures dressed in the colorful costumes of the various regions and classes of Poland.

Other amateur plays were based on Polish folklore, with a lot of music, singing, and dancing, but notwithstanding the fun, the plays usually had a basic moral. There were also more serious plays based on city life in Poland, or on Polish historical events or classics by non-Polish authors.

Soon the amateur theaters became so numerous and the choice of plays, written basically for the public in Poland, so inadequate and generally unsuitable for the Polish-American public, that new plays had to be written. The typical characters of the former folk theater in Poland, a Jewish tavern keeper, land estate owner, servile peasant, miller, blacksmith, chimney sweep, shoemaker, housemaid, and servant, had to be supplanted by characters typical to the new life in America and the plots had to be changed accordingly. The only exceptions were the Polish patriotic and historic plays and spectacles.

Among the most popular and most productive Polish-American playwrights was Anthony Jax (pseudonym) who, during the period from 1910 to 1920, wrote about fifty Polish-American theatrical plays. His, and similar, theatrical plays and Polish-American musical compositions were printed and sold mostly by the Sajewski Music House in Chicago.

The Semi-Professional Cultural Theater

Plays by foremost Polish and non-Polish playwrights were given usually by semiprofessional groups. Many Polish-American societies in the cities had, as a cultural project, the production of at least one stage play during a season.

By defining them as semiprofessional, I mean that most

participants in theatrical productions were amateur actors, plus professionals who were hired to supplement the cast or, vice versa, the amateur actors were asked to join a cast of professionals.

The cultural theatrical projects of the Polish-American clubs and societies embraced not only plays by Polish authors, but also works of Shakespeare, Moliere, Ibsen, Schiller, Gorki, and many other world-famous playwrights; naturally these were in Polish translation. They also included some operas and, on the lighter side, many operettas.

There were many attempts to organize a permanent Polish theater, strictly as a cultural institution, in Chicago and several other cities, with regularly scheduled performances to be given several times a week, or at least once a week. Such a theater was organized in one of the big downtown theaters in Chicago in 1906. It lasted about two years. Then a large theater building was rented in a Chicago Polish neighborhood, for the purpose of establishing a permanent Polish theater on a cultural level, but this attempt also failed. In the New York area, traveling Polish theaters on a higher level appeared once in a while and then folded up.

There were several attempts to interest one of the larger Polish fraternal organizations to finance a permanent traveling Polish theater as a cultural institution. These efforts were fruitless. Sporadic higher-level Polish theatrical productions including operas, sometimes with the participation of world-known Polish singers or dramatic artists from Poland, kept at least the semblance of a cultural Polish theater in America alive until the outbreak of World War II. In some communities, especially Milwaukee, Wis., where I succeeded in organizing the Polish Art Theatre Guild, Polish-American bilingual youth, interested in Polish culture and literature, presented some worthwhile theatrical productions of Polish plays in the Polish language.

Occasional Polish theatrical productions are still given in some cities of America; however, they are not produced by

Polish-Americans themselves—but are a product of the cultural exchange program of the United States and the government of Poland, for example, the fabulous Polish dancing ensembles, "Mazowsze" and "Slask."

The Early Polish-American Professional Theater

Among the hungry, unemployed Polish Bohemians, who came to America in the beginning of the twentieth century and tried to make a livelihood, there were many actors, singers, musicians, painters, etc., They were the nucleus of the Polish theatrical troupes, which were joined by others who loved the theater. Most of them had an additional occupation, as newspapermen, clerks, salesmen, and so on.

Their Polish professional theater was born in nickelodeons, on a stage behind the film screen, with dressing rooms attached or in the basement under the stage.

In between movies, a Polish play would be presented and, in addition, one of the actors or actresses would appear during intermission with a specially composed song, called a "couplet," which was sold among the public in the old theatrical vendor fashion. The profit from the sale of the song was an extra bonus for the actor or actress, and sometimes it amounted to more than the salary, which at the beginning was eight to ten dollars for a seven-day week. The theme of the song was based mostly on interesting recent events or a love story, bordering sometimes on the obscene.

With the addition of a Polish "live" show, the admission price to a nickelodeon was changed form five cents to ten cents, and later to fifteen, twenty-five, fifty-cents and up, until the combination of movies and "live" shows became unprofitable.

There were at one time twelve such Polish theaters in Chicago alone and many in other cities.

The Plays, The Public, The Actors

This was a repertory theater in the broadest sense. The plays changed three and sometimes even four times a week. Usually on Monday, Tuesday, and Wednesday evenings, there was a drama. On Thursdays, Fridays, and Saturdays, the play was of a comedy type, and on Sunday it was generally a slapstick farce or burlesque, minus the chorus girls. The Sunday public was composed of those who came to the theater to laugh and digest their Sunday dinner or supper.

Two performances were given on weekdays, but on Sunday there were six to eight performances and the actors had to suffer the heavy coat of greasepaint, nose putty, mascara, wigs, etc., from about noon to midnight.

The actors had to be versatile. Not only in the portrayal of various characters and parts, but they had to build, paint, and change the scenery, take care of the light and sound effects, make posters to advertise the plays and, sometimes, even make their own costumes.

The plays were partly adapted or shortened from plays written for theaters in Poland. Many others were written by the actors themselves, or translated and adapted partly or wholly from English, German, French, or other plays. The slapstick farces, given on Sunday, were full of improvisations by ad-libbing performers and cut in time, according to the wishes of the profit-conscious theater owner, whenever long lines were forming at the box office.

The nucleus of the professional troupe consisted usually of four or five actors and actresses and the prompter. The piano player, called the "professor," was cooperative in giving his accompaniment to songs and dances on the stage, but was not a part of the troupe. He belonged to the movies.

Amateurs and aspirants for professional acting were hired as extras; some were paid, some gave their talents gratis, and some even gave the director of the troupe a reward in money or gifts for the privilege of appearing on the stage, and being taught how to act with professionals.

The backstage was always a visiting place for lovers of the theater and art; for men whose wives didn't understand them; for those interested in a poker game; for newspaper writers and, in general, people who craved an occasional Bohemian atmosphere to break up the monotony of everyday life.

There were many severe critics of these professional Polish theaters and their performers. They would refer to them as cheap clowns and comedians. To be sure, these theaters had their faults and black sheep; but they also had many hard workers and idealists who tried to smuggle a little bit of joy, humor, and culture along with the entertainment.

One must remember that under conditions existing at that time, these theaters gave many Polish-Americans an opportunity to go, at a small cost, to a better place for relaxation than the prevailing saloon. The so-called comedians brought to homesick Polish-Americans memories of their homeland, with its music, songs, and dances and acquainted them with the popular American songs in Polish translation. They were responsible for creating an interest in the theater among many of those who had never seen a theater in Poland, and many of the young patrons of these Polish theaters later became active in dramatic clubs, giving Polish and English plays.

Polish-American Films

Later some of the Polish actors succeeded in organizing firms which produced silent films woven around Polish themes with Polish and English subtitles.

The most serious of such enterprises, in the twenties, was the production of the film *The Enchanted Circle* based on the Polish play *Zaczarowane Kolo* by Lucjan Rydel. Two of the most important parts were played by very well-known personalities in America. Adam Didur, basso of the New York Metropolitan Opera, played the part of Boruta, a Polish-type Mephistopheles. The part of the mighty Polish wojewoda (governor) was in the hands of Stanley Cyganiewicz, a world-known wrestler, older brother of another famous wrestler, popularly known in America as "Zbyszko."

There were also ingenious entrepreneurs who went into the production of Polish films based on the Middle Ages and on religious themes, to be shown in Polish parishes and halls. Some scenes were filmed in Chicago parks with knights in armor riding on old brewery horses; some in a small improvised studio. The expensive fighting and mob scenes, with glorious landscapes were cut from old American historical films, bought at a very inexpensive price and so, a "Polish" film was made in America.

In the late thirties some efforts were made to produce Polish films in Hollywood.

Polish Radio Programs

With the decline of Polish professional theaters in conjunction with movie houses, Polish actors got a new lease on life, partly in theatrical productions given on weekends on a larger scale in private or parish halls, and partly as participants or conductors of Polish radio programs. A few of them were lucky to get employment in Hollywood film productions.

Polish radio programs were quite popular for some time and were conducted not only by Polish actors, but also by other enterprising men and women and, unfortunately, by some who used very poor and ungrammatical Polish language.

These Polish radio programs, usually highly commercialized, were of different categories: some were conducted on a very low level; some on a higher one. Later some discontinued the use of the Polish language entirely, retaining only recorded or taped Polish music and songs. At one time, high level programs devoted to Polish culture were broadcast without the typical huckster-type commercial interruptions.

With more and more stringent rules and regulations governing foreign language radio programs and fewer people interested in hearing news, commercials, and soap operas in a foreign language, the original Polish programs began to disappear, but Polish music and songs, especially of the polka type, still have devoted listeners.

There are still some cities where the Polish language is used on radio programs, in news coverage and announcements, and there are occasional English-language TV programs with Polish-American entertainers in the Polish music, dance, and song field.

The old Polish-American theatrical world has come to its end, but performers of Polish-American stock are now more and more evident in another, the strictly American, world of entertaiment, theater, and related arts.

Of course, Polish-Americans had representation in this American artistic world a long time ago. For example, in 1876, a Polish actress, Helena Modrzejewska, came to California from Poland and won unanimous acclaim as a tragedienne of Shakespearean plays. She simplified her hard-to-pronounce Polish name to Modjeska. There is a monument in her honor in Anaheim, California and the Modjeska Ranch in her memory in the mountains of Santa Ana, California. She not only gave America her art, but also a son, Ralph Modjeski, the famous builder of important bridges in America.

We had and have many artists performing under theatrical names that do not disclose their Polish descent. For example, such glorified performers as Gilda Gray (Milwaukee-born Miss Michalski) of the Ziegfield Follies and Hollywood fame and Carole Landis (Miss Landowski) of the films and many, many others, too numerous to mention.

Today, many of them, although performing under non-Polish names, are not hiding their Polish descent, but disclosing it openly as in the case of the popular TV personality, Bobby Vinton.

Very often the Polish blood, temperament, and other characteristics, in one word, the Polish nature that they represent gives them a special "it" which they contribute to American culture.

X

Other Spheres of Polish-American Cultural Activities

Even in the cultural field, there was and is a lack of unity and co-operation among Polish-Americans, as evidenced by the rivalry between the several cultural institutions which claim to be working for the same cause.

The oldest and most outstanding is the Kosciuszko Foundation, organized in 1925 in New York by a Polish immigrant, who became a professor at Harvard University (as mentioned in Chapter VII).

At first he tried to form a scholarship committee, appealing primarily to Polish-American leaders. Being unsuccessful, with the support of Dr. MacCracken, president of Vassar College, he turned for help to several prominent Americans of non-Polish descent and with their help, was able to provide a solid foundation for a permanent Polish-American scholarship foundation, which established an American center for Polish culture in its own building at 15 East 65th Street in New York City.

The Kosciuszko Foundation is a small institution as compared with Jewish or German-American multimillion dollar foundations. Its solid assets were only over half a million dollars in 1964.

The yearly income from permanent funds, comprising profitable investments, augmented by yearly membership dues and donations has provided up to 1964 (the last time I saw their official report) the following:

1. Exchange of hundreds of students and scholars between Poland and America.

2. Hundreds of scholarships for studies in American institutions of higher learning, in the fields of Polish language and literature, music, and engineering. Most of the scholarships were restricted to students of Polish extraction, but some were given to students regardless of nationality, race, or religion.

3. Financial aid or valuable books to various Polish institutions and scholars in America, Poland, and other countries.

4. A clearinghouse of information, promotion of various cultural activities in America, and publishing of books, mostly in English on Polish topics.

Cultural-Minded Polish Immigrants

Some of the bequests received in the beginning by the Kosciuszko Foundation from Polish-American immigrants, who made good in America, are really inspiring and noteworthy.

One of them, Stanislaw Lesniak, came to America as a twenty-two-year-old youngster. Working hard, he saved enough money to enter an American university and became a prominent mining engineer and geologist. He changed his name to Stan Lesny and spent most of his life in the jungles of Mexico, Venezuela, and Colombia in the service of American companies looking for new oil fields. On the only photograph he left, besides the one in his passport, he is shown befriending a poor but large Mexican family.

When he died in 1956, he left his life's savings of over $130,000 for the purpose of establishing scholarships for

Polish-American students interested in "engineering and higher natural and social sciences classes as, the study of earth and man."

In another case, a Polish factory worker bequeathed to the Kosciuszko Foundation his life's savings of $25,000. A stockyard worker in Sioux City, Iowa left a bequest of $2,000. A widow of a Polish factory worker in Bristol, Conn. left $5,768.70, a university-educated man in Detroit left a bequest of $13,321. Similar bequests were made by other Polish immigrants interested in lifting Americans of Polish descent to a higher cultural level.

The William and Mildred Zelosky Scholarship Fund

The Kosciuszko Foundation was also connected with a project of exchanging students between Poland and America and vice versa in conjunction with the Zelosky scholarship fund, in the amount of about $600,000.

In the year 1963-64, seven students from Poland and three from America were to take part in this scholarship project.

This is another story of former Polish immigrants who made good in America and decided to use the money they made in this country to help people of their nationality to obtain a higher education and to promote mutual Polish-American understanding and friendship. Zelosky, who changed his name from Zelichowski, came to America as a thirteen-year-old boy in 1880. He was a farmer in Texas, a salesman in Chicago, and finally a successful real estate developer in that city. His wife's name was Warden, a simplification of the Polish Wardyn or Wardzinski. In the Polish-American circles in Chicago, they were not known as being of Polish nationality until the news of their testament was made public.

The Paderewski Foundation

Another Polish-American cultural institution was the Paderewski Foundation in New York, founded by a prosperous

Polish-American businessman, E. S. Witkowski, a close friend and associate of Paderewski. One of the aims of this foundation was to cultivate the memory of Paderewski as a great artist and statesman, just as the Kosciuszko Foundation wants to perpetuate the memory of the Polish general who fought for the independence of Poland and the United States, and for the emancipation of peasants in Poland and Negroes in America.

According to the last public report which I saw in 1964, the Paderewski Foundation had given, up to that time, 414 scholarships, amounting to $362,000 to Americans of Polish descent and Polish students, scholars, and artists, living in America and twenty-one countries abroad.

While the Kosciuszko Foundation was supported largely by former Polish immigrants who made good in America, the Paderewski Foundation had support from the higher American social and artistic strata and the Roman-Catholic clergy. Among the foremost personalities, whose names are connected with this institution, are many archbishops and bishops, governors of many states and, at one time, the vice-president of the Paderewski Foundation was F. Steinway, of the Steinway piano firm. Members of the Steinway family were known as Paderewski's close friends.

The Pulaski and Pilsudski Foundations

At the time when I wrote my original sketches in the Polish language in 1964, there were two other Polish-American cultural institutions in New York with the following aims:

The Pulaski Foundation claimed as its main objective the dissemination of information about Polish achievements, thus paying homage to General Casimir Pulaski, a Polish nobleman who gave his life for the United States in the Revolutionary War.

The Pilsudski Foundation wanted to pay homage to the Polish soldier and statesman, Joseph Pilsudski, by disseminating information pertaining to the role the Pilsudski movement played in history.

95

In addition, there were or are many lesser Polish-American cultural organizations; for example, the Polonaise Foundation in Chicago and various committees, collecting funds on their own, for scholarships and other educational purposes. The Polish-language press used to print news items about them with appeals for donations.

Scholars and Scientists and a Museum

Active on the university and college level is the Polish Institute of Arts and Sciences in America with headquarters in New York, comprising university professors, senior researchers, librarians, writers, and artists of Polish extraction. It maintains a large library, open to scholars; publishes books, pamphlets and an academic quarterly, *The Polish Review*. In 1964 it was compiling a register of scholars and scientists of Polish background in the United States.

The existence of a Polish-American Museum in Chicago was made known more widely to the American public some time ago with the news of a million-dollar robbery committed in this musuem. The gang of robbers was apprehended, but although most of the valuable articles were recovered, some are still missing.

Founded in 1935 as the "Archives and Museum of the Polish Roman-Catholic Union in America," it was changed to a secular organization under the name of the Polish Museum to represent the history of all Poles in America. After the robbery, efforts were made to collect funds for the erection of a separate building for this museum in Chicago. The exhibits in this museum were enriched by the art treasures from the Polish Pavilion at the New York World's Fair.

Polish Schools in America

These schools consist of two main categories: those conducted by religious bodies and those financed by secular organizations.

In the first category, the most important, as far as teaching of Polish language and culture is concerned, is the Polish Theological Seminary in Orchard Lake, Michigan. It was founded in 1884 by a Roman Catholic priest, Rev. Joseph Dabrowski, who was also an insurgent against the Russian Tsar and a printer.

He was responsible for bringing to this country the order of the Felician Sisters, recognized as outstanding teachers in Polish parochial schools, especially in the Polish language and related subjects.

Another religious organization, The Polish National Catholic Church in America, has a Polish seminary in Scranton, Pa., and its parishes conduct schools teaching the Polish language and history.

The highest secular school, financed mainly by the Polish National Alliance and individual contributions by its members, is Alliance College, founded in 1912 in Cambridge Springs, Pa. In 1914, a mechanical trades institution was added to the college in order to help and encourage Polish immigrants and their children to learn a trade. This institution was to cease its existence as of June 1965, but the four-year liberal arts college was to be expanded and a new dormitory was to be erected.

The area of Polish language and Slavonic studies was to receive special attention with the aim of "blending Slavic contributions into the mainstream of American culture."

In addition, there were and probably still are Polish departments in some state or private non-Catholic universities and colleges, public high schools, and elementary schools where Polish is still taught.

There are also some Saturday, Sunday, or vacation schools, conducted by various groups and organizations, devoted to teaching the Polish language, history, singing, and dancing.

There used to be many Polish lecture clubs, especially in Chicago, Detroit, and New York. Among them the educational society known as, "The Polish Peoples University" offering regular free admission lectures on Sundays, discussing various topics. This institution was organized in Chicago in 1895 and for some time it had two full-time paid lecturers, traveling from city to city.

Polish Arts Clubs

In the field of arts, music, and singing, some of the clubs prominent in 1964 were:

The remnants of the formerly numerous Polish music and singing societies, most of them now affiliated with the Alliance of Polish Singers, with headquarters in Chicago.

The Polish Arts Club in Chicago, which arranged every year a large-scale exhibit of the works of Polish artists.

The Polanie Club, Inc., in Minneapolis, Minn., publishers of many books, mostly in English, on Polish cultural topics. Among these books are *Treasured Polish Recipes for Americans,* and *Treasured Polish Songs with English Translation.*

The Polanki Club of Milwaukee, Wis., a Polish-American ladies' organization, similar to "Polanie" in Minneapolis, is active in acquainting the American public with Polish culture, especially traditions and preparation of Polish-style food. Some time ago this Club pledged $1,000 as its share for the erection of the Polish Museum in Chicago.

There are other similar clubs, most of them united with the Alliance of Polish Cultural Clubs, meeting together at yearly conventions in various cities. An organization of Polish doctors, dentists, and lawyers is affiliated with this Alliance of Cultural Clubs.

Among the more unique Polish-American cultural organizations, worthy of mention, is the "Polonus Philatelic Society" in Chicago, a club of collectors of Polish stamps. Sometime ago, when this Club opened an exhibit of Polish stamps and letters, from the early history of Poland to the latest era, the Governor of Illinois issued a proclamation, establishing the "Polonus Philatelic Day in Illinois."

And so Polish culture blends with American culture. And Polish blood blends with American blood, in various forms, as I have illustrated in these ten chapters.

In conclusion, to illustrate how this Polish blood gets into America's veins, I take the liberty to cite the following words of Senator Edmund S. Muskie of Maine (printed in the January 25, 1976 issue of *Family Weekly*, entitled "Is the Melting Pot Working and Should It?"):

"With only three Polish families in my hometown of Rumford, Me., I was distinctly in a minority. I can still remember the sting of such ethnic references as 'Polack.' I also remember the burning crosses of the Ku Klux Klan.

"My father gave me important advice. He told me to be proud of my strong Polish background but to think of myself as an American first. He was a tailor named Stephen Marciszewski, who came to America when he was 20. The reason he came was that *his* father was determined that he grow up in a free society.

"There is no conflict between America's 'melting pot' tradition and the preservation of my ethnic identity. The 'melting pot' distills the best traditions into something distinctly American.

"In my family today, we still talk about the customs and traditions of my parents because I enjoy them and associate them with fond memories of childhood."

(Sen. Muskie's statement is republished here with the permission of FAMILY WEEKLY).